507
Ways To Have Money

by
Will Green and Earl Strumpell

Bloomington, IN Milton Keynes, UK

authorHOUSE®

AuthorHouse™
1663 Liberty Drive, Suite 200
Bloomington, IN 47403
www.authorhouse.com
Phone: 1-800-839-8640

AuthorHouse™ UK Ltd.
500 Avebury Boulevard
Central Milton Keynes, MK9 2BE
www.authorhouse.co.uk
Phone: 08001974150

First published by AuthorHouse 3/19/2007

ISBN: 978-1-4259-9519-5 (e)
ISBN: 978-1-4259-9520-1 (sc)
ISBN: 978-1-4259-9518-8 (hc)

Library of Congress Control Number: 2007900833

Printed in the United States of America
Bloomington, Indiana

This book is printed on acid-free paper.

The authors and publishers do not assume and hereby disclaim any liability
to any party for any loss caused by errors, inaccuracies or omissions,
or injury resulting from the material in 507 Ways To Have Money.

We have done our best to acknowledge all sources and contributors. If we
have erred, please let us know and we will correct it in the next printing.

Cover Design by: Carol Weaver, the Pristine Agency
Editors: Valerie Frank and Valerie Goodman

Foreword

I got my first real job at 13 delivering the Washington Post newspaper between Massachusetts Avenue and Wisconsin Avenue in Washington, DC. The same year I added a second job delivering the Evening Star newspaper in the same neighborhood. Ironically, at the time I attended St. Alban's School, the National Cathedral School for Boys. Donald Graham, who today is the head of the Washington Post, was my class of '62 classmate.

Over the past 62 years I have made certain observations. Most of the really wealthy people I have known enjoyed several life-changing failures in their early years. My two mentors, both in the billionaire realm, each had third grade educations.

Both were philanthropic by the time I met them in their twilight years. Both understood that receiving required giving, and that the exchange determines the value of the encounter. Simply put, "give more to receive more."

I've been blessed beyond measure, and with barely a high school education, have earned many millions of dollars. It is more important to me that my friends and family prosper than it is that I prosper. Putting others first makes life more enjoyable and much more rewarding.

Here are my personal top 10 ways to have money. These are a little different than most of the ideas you might hear from my contemporaries:

I believe that all money I have belongs to God and He allows me to earn my portion by giving me ideas and supporting my efforts that are in line with His will. I believe in tithing and attribute much of my success to being blessed through this requirement of obedience.

My Personal Top 10 Ways to Have Money

1. The most important single way to have money is to tithe 10% or more to God's work and His purpose in your life. You must learn to ask the Holy Spirit to show you the areas He wants you to minister to. Support the ministries that spiritually feed you.

2. Find people less fortunate than you are and mentor them. To give of self is as important as giving money.

Mentor someone less fortunate than you are. Lift up another in a loving way. Show compassion to others.

3.   Get involved in helping a local ministry or charity feed the hungry in your town or city. Feeding the hungry encourages the same behavior in those closest to you. Expose yourself to life in the world around you and your own life will be more valuable to you.

4.   When you're in the grocery store behind an elderly person in the check-out line who is counting out coins from their change purse to pay for their food (this is an indication that they cannot afford to eat), give them a $10 or $20 bill and tell them God told you to bless them. What you do in His name for the good of others is multiplied back to you in multiples.

5.   Visit www.thewisdomcenter.tv and purchase the Uncommon Millionaire tape series. Dr Mike Murdock has one of the best teachings on prosperity I have ever experienced.

6.   Purchase classes, courses or seminars for you and your children that will expand your perception of life. Jay Abraham or Brian Tracy seminars, Nightingale-Conant audio tapes or CD courses will increase the prosperity

of your family. Learning never grows old and wisdom and knowledge increase your value to the world.

7. Dedicate Sunday, the first day of the week, to God as a day of rest and worship. Do business six days a week, not on Sunday. Spend this time with your family in praise and worship. God will bless you and your offspring.

8. Create a job for an elderly friend or neighbor that will help you save time and energy and allow them a little extra income. For example, they may like to fiddle in the garden with your flower beds, or help you organize your kitchen or office. When you bless someone else, God blesses you.

9. Give money to your children while you are still alive and healthy. Invest in them with both time and money. Plan a family vacation, cruise or trip and communicate with your children. You'll be amazed by what they teach you if you will just listen.

10. Celebrate Christmas with a Birthday Party for Jesus. Your family can celebrate God's greatest gift to man, His first born son, Jesus Christ.

How To Spend Less Money And Save More

All About Savings

"For you to accumulate real wealth, you must spend less than you earn and save or invest the difference for a long enough time to achieve compound growth."

Regardless of this simple yet profound fact that virtually guarantees wealth, most people think they will have to give up something in order to save and they don't do it. With a little careful planning, and some work in time and effort to find good deals on a consistent basis throughout your financial life, you can actually have more and save more at the same time.

The truth is you have to give up a lot more to not save. Let's take a look at some of the consequences of not saving and investing for the future:

No money for retirement

Not building up your savings and making investments for your future is a terrible way to live your life because it means that you are destined to the certain fate of an impoverished lifestyle when you retire. With no income and no savings for retirement, you are going to be dependent upon meager Social Security benefits and whatever retirement plan your company has given you, if any. Plus you will find yourself working in part time jobs just to have a roof over your head and get something to eat – if you can get someone to hire you.

For healthcare, you will have to turn to the over-burdened Medicare system just when you most want the best heath care for yourself and those you love. Older people without savings find that they are at the mercy of state and federal government facilities for medical care. They are given few options, and to make matters worse, the outlook in the future for quality geriatric health care is even bleaker than it is today. As the "baby-boomers" get older, they will place a burden on the health care system greater than at any time in our history. You don't want to be caught in the "system."

If you don't control your finances when you are young, someone else will control your life when you are old.

To put it bluntly, if you are of retirement age and you have no savings or investments, from the perspective of the time value of money - your time has run out! You won't get to make decisions about your life. Where you live, the kind of care you get, the people you have around you will all be at the mercy of your relations, or worse yet, government institutions and agencies. There could be some very uncomfortable years ahead for you unless you have provided for yourself. Time value of money is the ability of money to grow compounding over time exponentially.

No money for emergencies

Life is full of unexpected surprises: job loss, health problems, car breakdowns, accidents, pregnancy, disability, loss of a family member or loved one, natural disasters…to name just a few. We've all had them and they aren't going to go away. "Emergencies" happen to everyone and they happen on a fairly regular basis. Emergencies are a fact of life.

Whether you are a victim of crime or a victim of fate, the absolute best way to get through any emergency is to have a financial reserve, and that means savings.

Loss of personal freedoms

When you build up a substantial savings and investment portfolio, you will find that in life you have many more choices than those without wealth. As time goes by you can, for example, move to a nicer neighborhood, remodel your house, buy a vacation home, start your own business or change careers knowing you have a "reserve" that will see you through the transition from one circumstance to another.

Without savings you are stuck. Your options to change careers and find a better job are limited because you cannot afford to risk being out of a job. People without financial reserves have to be more cautious about work related decisions because they don't have a cushion. Being cautious, while appropriate, often limits the choices they have as to where they work and that ultimately has a huge impact on their wealth.

Everyone will experience several financial "opportunities" in their lifetime in the form of businesses that are for sale, real property being sold at distressed prices, or significant investment opportunities that are available to a limited few who can move quickly because they have ready cash. Only those who have wealth in the form of savings and investments will be able to take advantage of these opportunities. They are the few who enjoy the personal freedoms that financial independence offers.

It has never been more true than it is today: "wealth builds wealth; poverty breeds more poverty."

Difficulty financing and getting a good mortgage rate on your home.

When you buy real estate, it can be difficult to get a mortgage loan, or obtain a low interest rate on a mortgage loan when you have little or no down payment. If you can manage to save more than just a 20% down payment, you will have many more choices in the type of loan you get. You will experience much faster loan approval and enjoy better rates. In today's hot real estate market, when you do find your dream home, you have to move fast, because someone else wants it too. Without financial reserves, your ability to purchase and finance your "dream home" will be much more limited.

There is an old saying: "Banks only want to loan money to people who don't need it."

When you have no savings, your credit rating is at risk.

Without financial reserves in time of emergency, your financing options are limited, and you are going to go deeper into debt at ever higher rates of interest. You will have to reach deeper and deeper into the consumer credit market just to meet life's ongoing series of "emergencies." How many people do you know who go into debt to take a vacation, buy a car, or simply to give their family gifts for the holiday season? While these are terrible reasons to take on even more debt, many people do it without thinking. Credit cards and revolving credit accounts make it all too easy.

Without savings to cover emergencies, you can easily find yourself in a downward spiral of increasing debt. That won't happen when you have a savings reserve.

You can think of it this way: Every extra dollar you spend is a decision not to save. Every decision not to save is a step away from wealth and financial freedom, and into a life of limited personal freedoms, a circumstance that can easily be avoided. It takes discipline and strength of character, but the good news is, anyone can do it. Anyone, that is, who knows and adheres to the principle of the time value of money.

Do the Impossible: Save Money

Most people think that saving enough money to become wealthy is impossible. They think that people who are rich got lucky, won the lottery, robbed a bank, took advantage of someone, or resorted to less than legal means to acquire their wealth. While it's true that the "criminally wealthy" get mentioned in the news, the better truth is that hundreds

507 Ways To Have Money

of millionaires are made every day the good old fashioned way--with hard work, persistence and the principle of time value of money.

If you have been buying on credit, you are spending beyond your means. Remember, you must spend <u>less</u> than you earn, then save and invest the difference to create wealth. When you cut up your credit cards, you resist the temptation to spend <u>more</u> than you earn.

If you don't have a solid financial plan for getting your consumer credit paid off, feel free to consult with a professional credit counselor. You will find that many local governments have agencies that are free of charge and can help you organize your debt, get better rates, protect your credit, and get you out of consumer debt quickly and completely, forever. Do it now!

During your expected lifetime, the average American will earn millions of dollars in income. Let's look again at the following chart:

8	*hours*
5	*days/wk*
50	*weeks/yr*
35	*years*
70000	*total hours*

Hourly Rate	Lifetime Income
$10.00	$700,000.00
$15.00	$1,050,000.00
$20.00	$1,400,000.00
$25.00	$1,750,000.00
$30.00	$2,100,000.00
$40.00	$2,800,000.00
$50.00	$3,500,000.00
$60.00	$4,200,000.00
$75.00	$5,250,000.00
$100.00	$7,000,000.00

The big question is--how much of what you earn did you keep for yourself?

Saving is a discipline. You either have learned to be a saver from the time you were young, or you are of the "buy it now and pay for it later" crowd. There seems to be no middle ground. Savers build wealth while spenders lose theirs again and again. Savers are "spenders" too, because they "spend" their money on investments and opportunities that they know will help them get rich. Savers are motivated because they know they can build real wealth in their lifetime through the time value of money and compound growth, while spenders fall into a financial black hole as they take on more and more debt every year. You have a choice. If you have to spend, spend, spend your money, spend it on something that will either give you a good return or appreciate substantially in value. Every time you make a purchase you are making a decision about your financial future whether you realize it or not.

Saving and investing is an attitude and a belief that building wealth is more important than a moment of sensory gratification or having the latest electronic gadget or a snazzy new automobile. Saving is a daily decision to live modestly on less than what you earn. Every time you spend more than you know you should, you are making a decision to take away a big part of your future wealth.

Let's look at what that really means:

$100 savings invested just once with compound growth at 12% = $5,000 in approx. 35 years

$100 in savings invested each month for 35 years at 12% compound interest = $640,000!

That means that if you can save just $100 a month on any of your expenses, you will certainly have more money. You will accumulate real wealth by saving and investing the difference for compound growth, but only if you do it consistently. You have to make a decision, a promise to yourself that you will commit to this level of savings and investing each and every month for the next 35 years.

Exercise:

In the blank spaces, from the monthly expenses you are already paying now, every month, year in and year out, fill out the amount you believe you can <u>easily</u> save by following the suggestions we have given you in each of the seven areas:

Monthly

1. When I cut credit card debt I will save a monthly interest payment of .... $_____

2. By finding a better rate on telecommunications I will save .... $_____

3. By never paying retail for my purchases I will save .... $_____

4. By taking care of my health I will save .... $_____

5. By writing off my business related expenses I will save taxes of .... $_____

6. By constantly shopping for better insurance rates on car, home, property, and health insurance every month, I will save .... $_____

7. By keeping my utility bills in control I will save every month .... $_____

Total amount I commit to saving every month from the 7 expense areas: $_____

Now take that number, divide it by 100 and multiply times $640,000. That huge number is potentially the amount of wealth you can accumulate in 35 years by making simple, common sense changes in the way you spend your income on monthly expenses and investing the savings in long term investments that give you compound growth at 12% (which is, by the way, a very realistic return on <u>long term</u> investments).

_____ divided by 100 x $640,000 = $_____

My Commitment   **My Wealth**

If you could save just $25 dollars a month in four of seven areas you would save $100 a month and have over $640,000 in capital at the end of 35 years.

If you could save $50 dollars a month in just four of the seven areas, you would then be saving $200 a month, and you would accumulate $1,280,000 in capital during 35 years.

If you could save just $50 a month in six of the seven areas, you would be able to save and invest $300 a month leading to $1,920,000 in wealth at the end of 35 years.

Do you really believe you have to give up something of importance when you consider how much wealth you can actually accumulate by saving just a little every month? It's worth it!

There is absolutely no reason why anyone cannot accumulate serious wealth in their lifetime!

The Key to Saving is to Pay Yourself First

Now that you see how simple it is to control your expenses, there is no reason why you can't ***pay yourself first***. That means a minimum of 10% of every paycheck or every payment you receive in income should go directly to savings and investments. If you have completed the above exercise in the 7 expense areas, you probably realize 10% is too low. 20% is certainly feasible for almost anyone.

That means 20% right off the top of your paycheck and into savings and investments. This is a very practical and very rewarding way to build real wealth.

Exercise:

My current combined income is $\$$_____ per month. 10% savings "off the top" would mean that I am saving $\$$_____ every month.

$\$$_____ x 6,400 = $\$$_____ wealth in 35 years.

Monthly savings @ 10%

20% savings "off the top" would mean that I am saving $\$$_____ every month.

$\$$_____ x 6,400 = $\$$_____ wealth in 35 years.

Monthly savings @ 20%

Right here, right now I commit to saving _____% of my income every month.

Signed _____ Date_____

Change your mindset today towards savings, wealth, and ultimate success. In order to be successful you need two plans: a life plan and a financial plan. Unless you have a financial plan, you won't know where your money is coming from or where it's all going. Without a life plan it is very unlikely that you will live a rich and rewarding life on any level.

The first step in a financial plan is to start out with a budget. A budget is just a way to keep track of where your money comes from and where it goes. A budget is a system of accountability to keep you on track. When you work with a budget and you are tracking your income and your expenses, you can check in with your financial plan on a monthly basis. This "reality check-in" with your actual income and expenses vs. your budget can be highly motivating.

Remember, you are a "One-Person Financial Enterprise," ME, Inc. Every enterprise has a vision, goals and objectives, a unique market presence, and a set of strategies and tactics that help the enterprise stay on track towards its goal. For many people, their "strategies" and "tactics" are unconscious and they just can't see where they are going. View yourself as an enterprise and run your life like a business: your "profit" is the money you put into savings and investments.

It's not about how much you earn; it's about how much you keep.

You may find that you would benefit from professional advice, or you will want to read more books like this one on areas you are having trouble with. Find role models who will inspire you to do what they did to accumulate wealth.

Maybe your parents knew how to build wealth, or you know someone whose family accumulated wealth. Find out what they did and how they managed to get where they are, and then write your own story.

Writing your life story is a very powerful motivator. If you are having trouble getting into the idea of a budget or spending plan, then try this. Write two life stories for yourself. The first, you just keep doing what you've been doing for the next 5, 10, 20 or 50 years. Where are you at the end of your lifetime? Have you left a legacy or a disappointment? Are you an example, or a warning to future generations? Now write a second life story, one where you have a financial plan, a spending and investment plan, and you stick to it for the next 5, 10, 20 or 50 years. Where does you life story take you at the end of your "budgeted and investing" lifetime? Here's a better question – in which lifetime did you have more pain, more stress, more upsets, more tragedies, more disappointments, and more heartaches?

"If I would have known I was going to live this long, I would have taken better care of my teeth!"

Luckily, you don't have to do it all by yourself. As long as you actually save and invest, meaning as long as you *consistently accumulate capital,* there are tons of people and associations to help you grow your capital into real wealth. It's up to you to motivate yourself, find the resources you need, and make good use of them. And now the fun begins!

Why Save Money?

The number one reason to save money is to have money. Some people suffer under the illusion that they already have money just because they make a good income. That's way too short sighted and not very intelligent. It works great until you lose your job, and in no time you find yourself without any money at all. In other words, you are instantly broke. We'll say it again, "It's not how much you earn, it's how much you <u>keep</u> of what you earn that makes a difference."

Financial Security is When Your Money Works for You

Financial security is when you have enough money invested so that your money works harder for you than you do for your money. That's the very first goal of saving and investing, and it should be at the very top of your list of most important things to do. If those two sentences don't make sense to you, read them again and again until it sinks in.

What this means to you personally is that if you choose to take some time off from work, or if you find yourself suddenly unemployed for any reason, you will have enough income from your investments to sustain your current lifestyle, forever. It's really simple, and it's a concept that almost everyone knows about, but only the wealthy few have accomplished. How few? Less than 3% of the US population. The truth is, you can do it. We all can if we will do this one simple thing: take advantage of the time value of money. The principle is simple: spend less than you earn, save money and invest over the long term for compound growth.

If at this stage of your life you don't have any money working for you, then shame on you. No matter how young or how old you are, you need to have money invested. And if you are middle-aged or older and have no real savings or investments, it means for your whole life long you have been unwilling and/or unable to save. It means that when you get a paycheck, everyone gets paid but you.

When you save, it's like paying yourself first. If you don't pay yourself first, you will never, ever be wealthy. All of your earned money will go to buying things, paying taxes, and paying interest to your creditors. If this is what is true for you, then it's probably a good time to ask yourself "What is my long term financial plan?" If you don't have a plan, then you aren't going to be wealthy. Period.

The First Step to Savings and Investing is to Have a Plan

This is a scary proposition for many people. You have to actually think about where you are now, and where you are going financially. If you don't like to think about this, then you have company. Unfortunately, it's probably true that none of your like-minded friends are wealthy either. If you want to be wealthy, then you have to act like a wealthy person does and have a plan.

This kind of plan is really easy to think about because there are only three questions.

☑ Where are you now?

☑ Where do you want to be when you retire? (Broke or well-off?)

☑ What to you want to leave behind? (A legacy or a burden of debt?)

Now, all you have to do is to figure out how you are going to get there. Here's a simple plan for you to think about. The assumption is that you can actually save $100 a month and that you will earn, on average, a 12% return on your investments.

	Save Every		
Month	**10 years**	**20 years**	**30 years**
$100	$23,585	$96,838	$324,351

If you are 35 years old, and you plan to retire in thirty years at age 65, for every $100 a month you save, you will have an additional $324,351 in investments at retirement. That very same $324,351 in investments could give you an income of about $30,000 annually for the rest of your life if you make good investments. (We are assuming your investments return at approximately the same rate as the stock market has throughout it's history over any given five year period.)

So how hard is it to save $100 a month? That breaks down to about $3.25 a day. Do you think it would be possible to forego dining out once a week or buying a cup of coffee or a snack, so that you could save an average of $3.25 a day? You bet you can. Anyone can do it! Every single person in America can find a way to save $3 a day and become wealthier than 85% of all other Americans in the process. That's astounding!

It doesn't matter how much you make, it doesn't matter how much you have right now. All you have to do is decide to start saving. Right now.

Wealth is a Decision!

Do you know what this means? It means that the only difference between being wealthy and being broke is the decisions you make every day. You make wealth decisions every time you buy or don't buy a cup of coffee or a soda, and every time you take the bus or carpool to work, or put off buying a new car. The biggest decision you have to make is the decision to be wealthy, not poor. Yes, it is a decision. It's a choice. And only you can make it.

If you are like most people, you've already decided you are not going to be poor, and you make decisions each and every day consistent with not being poor. You know all about the phrase "spending yourself into the poorhouse." You have limits as to how far you will go – how many credit cards you will run up, how much credit you will take out, how much you will indulge yourself and how much you will spend to impress others. The problem is, you just aren't consciously aware of what you are ultimately doing with your life unless you have a plan. You are living a short term plan in a long term lifetime. And you can just as easily decide to become wealthy in your lifetime if you have a plan. First you decide, then you plan.

What if you were bold and adventurous and decided you could save two, three or ten times as much as you are saving now? Would that be difficult? Probably not, and we're going to prove that to you with our 500+ ways to save money in this book… and if you use even a small fraction of them, the exciting thing is you would have two, three or ten times as much money at retirement without ever getting another raise, without ever having to worry about how much you are spending on other things, or even how much you are paying in taxes!

Here's the best part. When you decide to invest a portion of your income in Investment Retirement Accounts (IRAs) you don't even have to pay income tax on the money you are putting away. You can truly "pay yourself first!" You don't have to pay taxes until you take the money out, and that means your money can compound and grow even faster! Then if you plan carefully for the future, when the time comes that you need to take the money out for retirement, you can pay substantially fewer taxes than you would pay on the same money today if you were to spend it. How great is this? If you want to save money, you don't have to pay taxes until you decide to spend it! The bottom line is that when money in an IRA compounds, the interest isn't taxed either! There is nothing standing between you and wealth. Not even taxes. You just have to decide to do it!

Home Equity is Not a Savings Account

Many people think that it's okay if they haven't got any money in savings because they have built up so much equity in their homes. This is another grand illusion of money and wealth that is shared by far too many less than wealthy people. It's seductive because it's a great feeling to believe you can go out and spend all of the money you earn and never have to worry about the future. No greater lie was ever told.

If you only think of your savings account as money that just sits there most of the time waiting for you draw on when you need it for special occasions like a medical emergency, or sudden unemployment, then granted, your home can be a source of money and you could think of it like savings. But that would be foolish. It is a serious mistake to think that way and here's why:

Savings is the money you use for investments, and investments are the source of investment income. When you have enough investment income, you won't have to work anymore. Your home is the place where you live. Unless you are into real estate investments and are comfortable "flipping" the home you live in, then your home is not an investment. First of all, it doesn't earn interest; instead it's an ongoing expense. "Yes it does earn interest," you say, "it appreciates in value, so that's just like a good investment!" Wrong!

Your home is where you live. Period. Just get over it. If you insist on thinking that home equity is as good as a savings account, ask yourself this question: Where are you going to live after you use up the "savings account" you call home equity? Are you going to step down to a smaller place, or become a renter? Do you know how hard that is? Most people, even those who have planned on doing just that at retirement, find it difficult if not impossible to step down from the home where they have lived for most of their lives for any number of reasons, not the least of which is the emotional and psychological hardship of giving up the comfort and familiarity of their home. This is especially true during a medical crisis!

Let's face it, moving all by itself is a life crisis. It's physically and emotionally draining to pack up all of your belongings, move into a less than desirable situation, and start all over again. It is really, really hard, if not impossible, for the elderly. If you look at your home equity as a savings account you can fall back on in time of crisis, you are asking for double trouble. Are you really prepared to have a medical crisis and know that at the same time you (or your spouse) will have to sell your home and move or dispose of all of your possessions? That's not financial security! That's a recipe for disaster. Please, please, please never think of your home equity as something you can "fall back on." Build wealth, leave a legacy. Be able to look back on your life with pride. It's amazing isn't it? The difference between wealth and destitution is just one decision. Your decision.

How To Save Money

Let us turn now to some common sense, simple, down to earth ways to save money that don't require that you sacrifice or give up anything.

Save Money in Your Financial Life

1. You're either a spender or a saver, there is no middle ground. You decide how your life is going to turn out financially every time you hold a dollar bill in your hand, use your ATM or credit card, or write a check. Save to spend, don't spend to save. If you are a spender by nature, spend all your money on good investments.

2. If both you and your spouse have investment accounts, bank accounts, or separate credit accounts, you can save on fees by combining them into one account.

3. If you and your spouse have more than one checking account you are wasting money. One joint account is all you need because that way you avoid fees associated with the extra accounts. It is also a great way for you and your spouse to work together on your financial goals since you will both have to know the checks and balances. Sound too difficult? They'll never do it? It would never work? Then you need to get into counseling because there are deeper issues in your relationship that will prevent you from ever becoming wealthy. No kidding!

4. Make sure you have "overdraft" protection on your checking account. The kind of service you want is a protection plan that transfers money from your savings account in case you overdraw your checking account. There will still be fees, but they will be much less than a regular overdraft charge and your check will be paid. You should have an automatic savings plan to back it up so there is always enough to cover any overages that may occur.

5. Don't keep big balances in your checking account. If your response to the statement above was, "I always keep more than enough in my account, I don't have to worry about that!" Then you are losing money.

Checking account funds are not invested. They don't work for you, you are working for them.

6.   If you are a senior citizen, ask your bank about special "senior" accounts and offers. You can often find accounts without fees or with reduced fees for seniors.

7.   Do you try to keep large bills, $100s or $50s, in your wallet in the hopes that you won't spend them? Are they for an "emergency?" How's that been working for you? If the answer is "not too well," try carrying a traveler's check instead. You'll have to sign it to cash it, so it is not as easily spent.

8.   If your ATM card gives you a source of "easy cash" then you need to cut it to shreds. Chronic and frequent cash withdrawals are a sure sign of overspending. Make it harder to get cash by doing without an ATM card. Absolutely don't use a credit card in its place! This is about developing a savings habit instead of a spending habit.

9.   Cut up your credit cards. Yes, you read it correctly. *Cut them up, NOW!* Keep only one for absolute emergencies and then pay it off as quickly as possible. Credit cards and consumer debt in the form of furniture, appliance, car or truck loans are the "black hole" of your wealth,

your neighbor's wealth, and our nation's wealth. It is financial gravity working against you and everyone else as the loan companies, banks, and credit card companies enjoy compound growth at your expense! Ouch!

10. Never play the lottery. The lottery is a "tax on people who are bad at math." Sure someone is going to win, but the odds are more than a million to one against you winning, and that's true every time you play. No exceptions. Worse than throwing away your money, the mental energy consumed fantasizing about winning is better directed to real goals that you can actually work to achieve. Statistics show that people who win the lottery end up right back where they were financially in just five years or less. It's better to earn it and own your financial success.

11. Take your biggest monthly expense and for just one day a month reduce it to zero. Turn off the water for a day. Use no electricity for a day. Use no heat or hot water for a day. Don't use the telephone for a day. Pay nothing for food for one day. Rent your house for a weekend and stay with a friend or relatives. Do whatever it takes to get an idea of what it would be like if your biggest expenses were reduced to zero. Think of the money you could save! This exercise, while inconvenient, will

inspire many new ways to save money as you find out just how resourceful you really are.

12. Spend a day helping the homeless by working in a shelter or with a charitable relief organization. You'll not only appreciate how much you already have from this experience, you'll find you can get by just fine spending much less money than you do now. It will really change your perspective about what's important in life. Besides, if you don't start saving and investing now, look at the lives of the people you are helping. That's how your life might end up someday. Here's a clue: financial security is everything! And the only way to have financial security is through saving and investing.

13. Who can you "network" with to save money? Business associates who share an office space, neighbors who share a run to the county dump, parents who car pool their kids are but a few examples of how you can save money networking with others. Grow your network of "saving buddies" as big as you can and watch your savings account grow exponentially.

14. To save money on rent, or to supplement your income to pay down your mortgage, consider renting out that "extra" room in your house. If you have a "granny unit" that is unoccupied, a little fixing up can bring

you a handsome rental. Consider it your first "income property." You might want to consider adding on, or converting the basement or garage for this purpose. Calculate the Return On Investment and see if it makes sense. Most importantly, it will get you to start thinking about and enjoying passive income.

Save Money on Groceries and Household Items

15. The average family spends $600 - $1000 a month on food and sundries. By shopping at club stores, using discount coupons, and buying in quantity when items are on sale, that number can easily be reduced by up to 20% or even more without giving anything up at all in terms of how much food you have or how well you live.

16. Reduce impulse buying at the grocery store by leaving the kids at home.

17. Never shop when you are hungry.

18. Always shop from a list. That means buying only those items on the list and no more. If you forgot to put it on the list, you don't need it. Take a calculator with you and stick to your budget.

19. Avoid buying prepared, pre-packaged, or processed foods and ready-to-eat meals. These items may be "time savers" but they cost you plenty. Look for the "price per serving" and compare; you will be shocked at how much you are paying for convenience. Besides, it's healthier to eat foods that are prepared from scratch because only then can you control the fat and sodium levels in your diet. Ironically, healthful food that is good for you is much cheaper than processed food.

20. Cutting back on your meat and dairy consumption not only will save you hundreds of dollars every year, but your family's health will be improved as well and you will save on health care expenses.

21. Cutting back or eliminating your consumption of tobacco and alcohol products can save a fortune every year. Cheaper healthcare in your lifetime? You shouldn't have to even think about this one.

22. Stock up on frozen foods at the end of the season. A good example: frozen turkey is much cheaper just after the holidays. You can buy and freeze many items yourself and save money because you get them when they are plentiful. Strawberries in season are another example. Do remember to use them up within a few

months: most frozen foods lose all their quality after one year in the freezer.

23. Always buy generic or store branded items that are cheaper than the national brands. If the ingredients are the same, the product is the same. Don't be stupid and pay a higher price for the exactly the same thing just because it's got a brand name on it.

24. Pay attention to the "per unit" price and you'll pay less at the register. It's not uncommon for smaller sizes to cost less per unit even through most people think the larger size is always cheaper.

25. Watch for coupons and special offers on the types of food you buy most often. Stock up when they are on sale.

26. Keep your grocery receipts with the coupons on the back in your wallet and present them with your money for on-going savings on the products you buy most.

27. Don't drive all over town to save just a few cents on a carton of milk. The money you spend on gas to get there far outweighs any savings. Try to find one or two stores, three at most, where you know you get good prices and that are conveniently located.

28. Buy any non-perishable items available in bulk at a warehouse store once a month and purchase perishable food like bakery goods, meat and produce at the lowest priced local grocer close to your home and only as you need them.

29. Remember to always shop with a list at warehouse stores; they really tempt you with their great prices, and you can easily find yourself buying too much or too many of products you don't really need. Remember, a bargain is only a bargain if you can use it!

30. If your community has a farmers market, keep in mind how much you are paying for similar items at the grocery store and look for bargains, but don't be fooled into thinking everything is cheaper at a farmer's market, because it isn't. The real bargain at a farmer's market is the freshness and the quality of what you are buying... and many times it *is* cheaper.

31. When you buy groceries, pay attention to the expiration date. Often you can find fresher items in the back of the display case. They will last longer, saving you having to throw out expired food.

32. If your grocery store chronically offers goods that are at or near the expiration date, find a new place to shop.

Fresher is always cheaper. Nothing is more wasteful than perishables that spoil a day or two after you buy them. You just end up throwing them out. You can tell when a store prides itself on fresh produce-that's where you want to shop even if their prices are a little higher.

33. Use olive oil instead of butter – it's cheaper than butter and it tastes just as good.

34. Grow your own herbs for seasoning… use a window box in winter, a garden plot the rest of the year, and you'll have fresh herbs all year long saving you a ton of money. Fresh herbs are the most expensive produce in the grocery store, and at the same time they are very easy to grow yourself.

35. Store leftovers in old margarine or other kinds of re-sealable containers and avoid the expense of high priced Tupperware or similar products.

36. Buy products that come in canning jars that can be reused to preserve food (be sure to sterilize the jars before using them again).

37. When you store food in your refrigerator, always used covered containers. Your food will stay fresher longer and taste better too.

38. Never store food that is still warm. Uncovered, warm foods not only give off heat, they give off humidity, and that makes your refrigerator work much harder and wastes energy.

Save Money on Telephone Expenses:

39. It pays to do your homework – the average household spends over $960 annually on telecommunications. With a little research and not too much time invested, you can easily cut that in half. Get out all of your telecom bills and work on the biggest expenses first.

40. You need to consistently control telecom expenses or they will wreck your financial plans and ultimately your wealth. Remember what just $50 a month can mean to your future wealth! What would it mean to you if you could save half of what you spend on telecommunications every month? It's not that hard.

41. Know how much you are paying per minute after all the taxes and surcharges are added in. You would be amazed at how much variation there is in the actual bottom line cost per minute. For example, a long distance carrier may advertise 3.9 cents per minute, but when you get the bill and they've added all the service charges, taxes and fees, you've actually paid more than 12 cents a

minute. To find your bottom line cost per minute, take the amount due and divide it by the total minutes you've used. You need to do this for all of your phone service, land lines, and cell phones.

42. Shop around for a better long distance rate every two or three months. Don't you hate getting phone bills? They're always higher than you expect and never what you wanted them to be. The only way to keep phone costs down is to stay on top of exactly how much your carrier is charging you and then look for better rates. Be sure to get the "bottom line" cost per minute! (Although we admit it can be difficult to get them to discuss surcharges, service charges and taxes. Ask for a supervisor if you have to.)

43. Try to find smaller, lesser known long-distance providers. Often you will get the best long-distance rates if you look harder. There are thousands of discount-rate small companies who don't have the big ad budgets but you may have to work harder to find them. Look for newspaper ads, yellow page ads, and research the internet for the best deals. You might check out www. phonecallworld.com for more ideas, or Google search "long distance telephone."

44. There are two different long distance rates: interstate and intrastate. If you make most of your long distance calls within your state, try to find the provider with the lowest intrastate rates. If your long distance calls are out of state, look for the low cost interstate provider. Better yet, use lowest cost providers for each type of service.

45. Cell phone bills can be shocking. That's because you're on a monthly allotment of minutes that almost everyone goes over at one time or another. It takes work to get a plan where you are not buying too many minutes and you are not going over your limit (if that's even mathematically possible!). A better solution is to get a prepaid phone. These can be purchased with rates as low as 10 cents a minute (T-mobile) and there are never any monthly service fees, taxes, or overage charges. If you are paying more than 10 cents a minute on the bottom line per minute cost for your cell phone (and that's almost everyone!), switch to a prepaid plan. An added bonus is that you will never get an unpleasant surprise at the end of the month. In fact, you won't even get a bill.

46. Compare the bottom line long distance rates for your land line phone to the bottom line rate of your cell phone. In many cases its cheaper to not have a long

distance plan on your land line, and if that's the case, you'll only want to make long distance calls on your cell phone. Don't forget the advantage of land lines is that you can still receive incoming long distance and local calls for free. If someone calls in on your cell number, ask them to call back on your land line.

47. Look on your phone bill to see if you are paying for any "extras." Call the provider and get them to take off extemporaneous services like inside wiring, voicemail, caller id, three-way calling and call waiting. These really add up in a year's time and they simply are not necessary or even useful. Take them off now!

48. Consider turning off your land line phone and only having a cell phone. There is always a monthly basic services cost for your land line phone, even if you hardly use it. If you find you are having a reaction to the thought of "no land line" in your home (What if there's an emergency?)- get over it! In case of natural disasters, cell phones are better because when the power's out and/or the land lines are down, your land line phone is useless. The technical term is "dead." Cell phone providers have a much better record of providing uninterrupted service in disasters – of course this doesn't apply if you live where there is no cell phone service!

49. If you travel and stay in hotels, never use the hotel's phone system to make calls; use your cell phone. Hotel phone charges can be extraordinarily high for the minutes you use.

50. Get rid of any unnecessary phone lines and cell phones. Most people have way more phones than they need. If you, your spouse, and all of your kids have a cell phone and you have two land lines and a fax line in your home, you are wasting tons of money on telephones every month.

51. Be sure to check out "family plans" if you have more than one cell phone in your household.

52. Team up with other family members who live in the same area, or get your co-workers, friends or neighbors to go in with you on a "family plan." With these types of arrangements, you'll definitely want unlimited minutes so that there are no disputes over who used too many minutes! But this can work and will save you significant dollars in some situations, even if they aren't your "real family."

53. If you aren't a big long-distance user, drop long distance service from your land line and use a phone card instead. Phone cards have advantages similar to a prepaid cell

phone, no taxes, fees and service charges will be added to the per minute cost, and you'll never be surprised by a big long distance bill.

54. Long distance and cell phone companies charge by the minute, but what happens if you talk for a minute and 20 seconds? This is called "call rounding" and you need to know how your long distance carrier and your cell phone company bills in order to get the best per-minute rates. It's another thing to ask about when you are calling around for better rates. Smaller long distance phone companies use six second rounding, and that means you are billed in six second increments. Many cell phone companies use "minute rounding." For example, you will be charged for two minutes even when you actually use just one minute and two seconds of time. It doesn't sound like a big deal, but it adds up. Six second rounding means that you would have been charged one minute and six seconds for the same call.

55. Use e-billing if it saves you money. Many carriers will offer you a discount if you receive your bill through your email and pay your bill on-line.

56. Use automatic payment plans, but only if you get a discounted rate for it. You probably should have some automatic bill paying set up with your bank (as long

as it's free), but it only makes sense to use this for your phone or utility bills if you get a discount.

57. Telephone and utility companies can change billing cycles and due dates by as much as 10 days, so you really have to watch out. Late fees add unnecessary expenses to your phone and utility bills. Of course, always pay your bills on time, and remember, watch out for changing due dates!

58. If your phone company offers digital cable, high speed internet, long distance and local phone service, be sure to check out their "package" prices and carefully compare them to buying from individual providers. These providers of telecom "packages" tend to run the services together on one bill. You need to realize that there is a hidden cost - it takes more work to monitor costs of each part of the package. If the cost of just one service on the "package pricing" changes to your detriment, it will be more difficult to do anything about it because the package pricing will no longer apply and everything has to be recalculated. Yes, it's complicated and they like it that way, because it means you are less likely to switch.

59. Extreme savings tip – maximum savings comes from having only one phone and no cable or internet. In

fact, all you need is a pre-paid cell phone that you use as little as possible… and no land line phone! Get a prepaid phone card and use a pay phone to make calls when or where your cell phone doesn't get reception.

If you have to have phones, cable and/or internet, you can cut your expenses by shopping around for better communications rates – every month! Telephone services are one of the most out of control expenses for consumers. Today we have cell phones, land lines, fax lines, internet connections, and cable TV all wrapped up in one telecommunications service. The choices are staggering and the differences between plans can make the difference between having money left to save, or not.

60. If your cell phone bill is always more than the dollar amount of the plan you thought you signed up for, try using a prepaid cell phone service. In that way you can never spend over your limit.

61. If you have to have cable TV, buy just the basic service and rent movies from the video store. Compare to learn if basic satellite is cheaper than cable in your area.

Save Money on Utilities

62. Typically about 60% of a household's energy bill goes towards heating and cooling. Focus on energy savings there first. Water heating comes in at about 20%. Cooking and refrigeration account for just 10%; lighting and small appliances make up the remaining 10%.

63. Always check the energy guide when you buy any appliance, small or large. A cheap appliance that uses a lot of "watts" is more expensive than a higher priced energy efficient model, by far. Any appliance that produces heat consumes a lot of energy, and its energy usage numbers deserve your full attention.

64. To figure the costs of energy consumed by an appliance, you can use your energy bill and the wattage figure from the appliance. First find out how much you pay for a kilowatt hour. Actually this figure is usually expressed as a cost per kilowatt hour, a "kilowatt hour" meaning 1,000 watts for an hour. For example, if you are buying a hair dryer that is rated at 1,000 watts, your kilowatt hour rate in dollars will tell you how much it costs to run the hairdryer for an hour.

65. Make sure you know where to turn off all the utilities coming into your property-electricity, gas, water,

propane, heating oil, and so forth. Have the tools you will need for each task nearby. Keep the area around each shut-off clear of weeds, brush, and debris. Clearly mark each one with colored paint and teach your family where they are and how to shut them off. If a pipe should burst, or a wire short out, being prepared to cut off the supply of water, gas or electricity in a hurry can be a real life saver.

66. If the top of your water heater is exposed, insulating the pipes and covering the top of the water heater itself with insulation will conserve energy. You need more than just a "blanket."

67. Get used to using less hot water for showers by making them shorter; install restrictors to reduce flow in all your shower heads.

68. There are new water heaters with a plastic (polymer) liners that are guaranteed to never leak and are more energy efficient. If you are replacing your water heater, be sure to consider the energy costs and take advantage of any rebates available through your utility company for the energy saving models.

69. To find the most efficient water heater pay attention to the FHR (First Hour Rating) and the EF (Energy

Factor). Larger water heaters lose energy faster; smaller heaters always have a better EF. Only buy as much capacity as you need.

70. Move your water heater closer to where you need hot water; normally that means the bathrooms at the bedroom end of the house. If your water heater is located on the other side of the house from your bathrooms, then you are wasting water and energy. At least get under the house and insulate exposed hot water pipes wherever possible.

71. If your water heater produces more than 120 degrees at the tap, it's turned up too high. Some people think hotter water kills more germs. Sterilization requires boiling in water for more than 20 minutes. Save your hot water bills and turn your water heater down to a thermometer-measured 120 degrees at the tap. You can use a meat or cooking thermometer for this purpose.

    If you find that when you turn your hot water down to 120 degrees the water is not hot enough in some areas of your home that means you are losing heat someplace – check under the house for exposed hot water pipes and insulate them as much as possible. Try to solve the heat loss problem before you turn the temperature back up.

72. If your laundry room or kitchen is on the other side of the house from the bathrooms, you may want to install a second smaller water heater. Two small water heaters use less energy than one big one because the use is closer to the source and less energy is lost in transmission. Smaller water heaters are more efficient, too.

73. Fix leaky faucets, hose bibs, sprinkler systems, and kitchen and bath fixtures. A slowly dripping faucet or hose bib in the garden can waste hundreds of gallons of water a year. Sprinkler systems that run under ground often leak where you can't see them. The only way you are going to know is to turn off everything and look to see if your water meter is turning. Wait an hour or two and come back to see if the needle has moved. If there is any movement, no matter how small, that means you've got a leak somewhere.

74. Instead of buying water from the local utility, see if you can put in a well. Another option is to divert the flow from a nearby river or stream, or simply capture rainwater runoff in a pond, tank, or catch basin so you can use the water for your garden, lawns, pets, or livestock without having to pay the utility for it.

75. If you have to wait a long time for hot water, use an under-sink hot water circulator. A hot water circulator

hooks up under your sink and diverts the hot water feed back into the system until a suitable temperature is reached. The electricity costs about $2 a year to run it, but it will save you a lot of water (up to 16,000 gals a year per faucet or shower).

76. Install a temperature sensitive faucet in your shower. These devices will quickly adjust the temperature so you can stop waiting for the right temperature.

77. If you can't spare the expense of a temperature sensing shower head, here is a cheaper way to accomplish almost the same thing. Adjust the "maximum" hot setting on your existing shower control to a maximum that's about what you like for a shower, maybe just a little higher, but not much. You may need to get your plumber to do this for you on their next visit. You'll save because you won't waste hot water fiddling around to finally get the temperature "just right."

78. As the shower adjusts to the right temperature, catch the "it's too cold" water in a bucket and use it to water plants and garden.

79. Most women shave their legs in the shower or tub. Men can shave their face in the shower, too. You can do it by feel, or get a fog resistant mirror at the hardware store

or a bath specialty shop and do your shaving when you lather up in the shower. You'll save the hot water you would have run in the sink. You do turn off the water as you lather up, wash and shave, don't you?

80. Most of your water is used in the bathrooms. Take showers instead of baths and you'll save on hot water as well. A bath takes about 30 gallons; a five minute shower taken at low flow rates uses as little as 10 gallons, even less if you turn the water off to lather up and wash.

81. After a shower do you throw towels in the hamper? Save the energy it takes to wash and dry towels so often by hanging them up to dry in the bathroom for your next shower. You will get two or three uses before you finally have to wash them, cutting your energy use in half or third.

82. When you wash dishes by hand, do you leave the rinse water running constantly? This wastes both water and heat. If you need to wash a large pot or vessel, do it first and then fill it with clean rinse water. As you wash, run your dishes through the rinse water without running the faucet all the time. After rinsing, let them air dry in a rack, saving time and effort, you won't have to wash so many towels.

83. Can you boil water faster using hot water from the faucet instead of cold? Yes, indeed-it's just physics after all. Hot water boils faster than cold water. The problem is that it costs a lot more to heat water in a water heater and pipe it to your kitchen than it does to boil it on your stove. So please start with cold water from the tap when you want boiling water in the kitchen. (It will taste better too; water heaters and hot water pipes tend to have a "flavor" most people find undesirable in their cooking.)

84. Cover the pot when you want to boil water. The cover keeps in the heat and the water will come up to a boil that much faster.

85. When you want to boil water, turning the burner up half way will save energy and you will hardly notice that it takes just a little bit longer for the water to boil. A burner turned up to its highest setting puts out a lot of heat that never gets into the pot or pan.

86. In hot weather, use a soaker hose instead of a sprinkler. A sprinkler allows water to evaporate up in the air before it even hits the ground.

87. In hot weather, run your sprinkler system only at night to get the most efficient watering of plants and lawns

by reducing evaporation. (You do use a drip system wherever you can, right?)

88. If you wash dishes by hand, let them air dry in winter, towel dry in summer and hang out the towels to dry.

89. Remember you can use dish water in your garden when you're done. It's called "gray water" and is safe for use on lawns and plants as long as there isn't too much soap in it.

90. Soft water saves your clothes from premature wear and requires less soap. If you have really hard water, get a water softener – it will save you money in the long run.

91. Never start your shower by running all "hot" water and then cutting in some cold. This wastes tons of hot water. Start with a setting close to where you know you like it from the beginning and let the temperature come up as you get into the shower. It may feel a bit cool in the beginning of your shower but energy-wise it's much more efficient.

92. In winter the cold water coming into your toilet soaks up a lot of room heat. At the same time the cold water keeps the bacteria count down (it won't get so "smelly" to put it bluntly) so you don't have to flush as often.

Not flushing when you use the toilet (unless you really must) saves both energy and water. Do it more often in the cold winter months.

93. Put a brick in your toilet's water tank to use less water when you flush. You can try adjusting the float ball for the same effect. Be sure the toilet still flushes well so you don't have to double flush all the time or your savings will be lost.

94. If your toilet doesn't flush well, check "under the hood" and make sure everything is working. If you have hard water, be sure to check the flush jet for proper operation. Hard water calcifies inside the jet and that needs to be removed. If you have to flush twice, it uses twice as much water.

95. Some dishwashers have a setting to delay the onset of the wash for 2, 4 or 6 hours. Time your dishwasher to run at night, especially during the summer months when the heat and humidity from the dishwasher will have a reduced effect on your comfort so you can keep that thermostat on an economy setting all day long.

96. A new dishwasher can more than pay for itself in energy savings, plus you no longer need to pre-rinse, as most all new dishwashers have a "hard food" disposer built

in. Not only do you save labor, time and energy, you save precious hot water.

97.	During hot weather if you run your dishwasher at night, open it in the morning after it has cooled down so you don't release a burst of hot, humid air into your house. Do the opposite in cold weather.

98.	If you have an older gas stove with always-on pilots, turn off the ones for the burners you don't use often and keep a hand-held lighter handy for when you do want to use them. Or, better yet, install electric starters on all of your burners and turn the pilots off altogether.

99.	You can use a professional style "restaurant" stove without using more energy. In fact, they often are more efficient because with a larger burner they heat water faster and more efficiently at lower settings. Just be sure that the stove has smaller burners as they are more efficient for your smaller pots and pans.

100.	Professional chefs use gas burners, but they switched to electric convection ovens because they bake more "evenly" and the food bakes faster, saving energy and time.

101.	If you like the "retro" look in kitchen appliances, you aren't stuck with energy inefficiency. Today, many manufacturers build energy efficient units in the "retro" style.

102. If your kitchen is cold on winter mornings, never use the oven or stove to warm the room. This is a terrible waste of energy. Use a small portable floor heater instead and leave the stove and oven for cooking.

103. Check your oven door gasket for wear or damage. A leaking oven door wastes energy by letting heat escape.

104. Keeping your refrigerator or freezer too cold wastes electricity. The recommended refrigerator temperature is 38 to 40 degrees. The recommended temperature for the freezer compartment is 5 degrees. If you have a separate freezer for long-term food storage, it should be maintained at a cooler 0 to -5 degrees.

105. Check the gaskets on your refrigerator door and freezer door for the same reason. Leaks waste energy on both sides of the appliance and cost you money.

106. Refrigerator gaskets have magnets inside them to help hold the seal against the jam. If you keep the surfaces on your refrigerator clean, the magnets work better and the seal will be tighter, keeping in more of the cold air.

107. Adjust your refrigerator with the help of a carpenter's level so that the doors close automatically (the feet on the bottom are really large screws that raise or lower each corner of the refrigerator). By raising the front of the refrigerator, you can cause the doors to close with greater force. Your refrigerator won't accidentally be left open and wasting energy by trying to refrigerate your whole house.

108. Keep your freezer at least half full. Refrigerators push air through the freezer first. When you open the freezer, the coldest air is lost quickly. If you don't have much frozen food, use bags filled with water or freezer blocks. Should your power go off, the cold mass of frozen water will help keep your frozen food frozen much longer.

109. Organize your refrigerator so you can find what you need quickly. Less time with the door open saves money. Teach your kids to put their stuff in the same place every time so they can find it quickly and get the door shut. With better organization food won't get lost and spoiled, and you'll save on groceries. Put the things you use most often in the door or towards the front so you can find them easily.

110. During hot weather be sure to pull out your refrigerator a couple more inches from the wall and give it a little more

room to "breathe." Efficiency can go up dramatically, especially if your refrigerator is enclosed on three sides by cabinetry. Even so, you might want to see if there is a way to open up the area behind the refrigerator.

111. Front loading washing machines use less water and are more energy efficient. If you are even close to needing a new machine, check out the advantages to your budget over the long term. Be sure to check for rebates from your local utility for the energy efficient models. You may be able to afford that new washer or dryer sooner than you thought.

112. Read this ONLY if you have an ELECTRIC clothes dryer: In the colder winter months you can switch over your outside vent to let that warm, humid air that comes out of your dryer into your house. You will want to use a special vent screen, available at hardware stores and home improvement centers, to keep the place from being covered with lint and dust. Please, NEVER try this with a GAS dryer!

113. If you can find a place to do it, run a clothes line and dry your clothes indoors when it's really cold and the air outside is dry. The water evaporating from your clothes will add to the humidity in your house and you will be more comfortable--meaning you'll save on your heating

bill when you turn your thermostat down a notch or two as a result.

114. After you take a shower, don't throw your towel in the hamper after just one use. Instead, hang it back up and let it dry out for the next time. Frequent washing and drying of towels wears them out quickly and consumes a lot of energy. You were clean when you got out of the shower, right? So your towel shouldn't get "dirty" after just one use. If you are really sensitive, keep a smaller "face towel" nearby for one time use, use a bath towel for the rest of your body, and dry your feet on a mat.

115. When you do wash your towels in the laundry, be sure to mix them with other laundry. Nothing is harder on your dryer than a mass of towels all tangled together. When you mix the load, it tends to keep towels separated and they dry faster, saving you energy, and your towels will last longer, too.

116. The best place for a clothes washer and dryer is outside your house in a utility room so that the heat and humidity from doing laundry doesn't affect the climate in your house.

117. Since towels are the most difficult items to dry in your clothes dryer, let them dry out on a rack or line, and

then put them in the dryer while still slightly moist, for that "fluffy" feeling.

118. Lighter weight clothes will get baked out when put in the dryer with towels, so save your clothes by only drying towels together with clothing of similar weight like jeans and pants.

119. Always run your dryer full of clothes for maximum efficiency. Too many clothes, however, reduces efficiency dramatically.

120. Same for the washing machine. Full loads are most efficient, but if you put in too many clothes they just clog together and don't get clean. Too-heavy loads (towels, rugs, etc.) may damage your machine, so you want to mix them with lighter clothes, or wash them by themselves.

121. Elastics are damaged by the heat of the clothes dryer. Ladies' underwear is especially vulnerable to dryer heat and should only be air-dried on a rack or line.

122. Be sure to frequently check the hose that comes out of the back of your dryer and the vent that pipes dryer exhaust to the outside. When they get clogged up with lint (it's inevitable) you'll need to pull out the dryer, disconnect the hose and clean out all the lint. A plugged

up hose and vent makes for a very expensive (and time consuming) clothes drying experience. You'll know your vent is plugged when your clothes take forever to dry.

123. You might want to relocate your dryer and/or the exhaust vent to get the shortest hot air exhaust route. The fewer the number of bends, and the shorter the pipe, the less frequently it will clog up, and that will make your life a whole lot easier.

124. Towels tend to ball up and wrap themselves around each other in the dryer, so throw in a mesh net to keep them separated.

125. When you dry shirts and pants be sure to take them right out of the dryer. Hang them up or fold and smooth out any wrinkles while they are still warm, and you won't have to iron them.

126. Wash your clothes in cold water and save up to 60% of the cost of washing your clothes. Most detergents work just fine in cold water.

127. Gas clothes dryers are more efficient than electric dryers. Even if you have to get a gas line run to your laundry room, it's almost always worth it to switch from electric to gas.

128. The best time to buy a new air conditioner is when they are on sale in the winter months; the best time to buy a new heater is during the spring and summer when they go on sale.

129. If you have a HVAC system, your thermostat may automatically switch from heating to cooling (especially in fall months with cold mornings, warm afternoons). This is good for comfort, bad for energy. Using only one mode saves energy; you will have to decide based on weather and time of year how to set your system.

130. Standing water is bad in summer because it raises humidity and that makes your cooling system work that much harder. Cooking pots and pans, cups, saucers, flower pots, plants, even the kitchen sink are all possible sources of standing water. In winter, you want more humidity for comfort, so the opposite applies.

131. Electronic or digital thermostats can allow you to fine tune your heating and cooling system. Most allow you to set temperatures for different times of day, on any day of the week. It makes sense and will save you many dollars to set temperatures lower in winter, higher in summer, especially during those times each day when no one is home.

132. Really sophisticated electronic thermostats sense temperatures both inside and outside your home. These are called "smart" thermostats because they anticipate your needs. For example, if it's really cold outside, they will start the furnace earlier and raise the temperature slightly to compensate. You will be more comfortable, and that means no one is going to have to turn the thermostat "way up" to take off the chill.

133. Your HVAC system has dampers or vents in each room. Close off the dampers in rooms that you aren't using. At night, close off all dampers except for those in occupied bedrooms. This works best if the thermostat is located in the same part of the house where you sleep.

134. Adjust the air dampers on your HVAC system to "balance" the temperatures in your house for efficiency. If some rooms are warmer than you want, and others stay cooler, that's a sign you need to balance your system. Call a HVAC professional if you need help.

135. Humidity makes the air feel warmer. If you use an air conditioner it will dry the air as it works. Don't fight your air conditioner by leaving standing water in sinks, pots, glasses, or other containers. Close the bathroom door and open a window when you get out of the shower.

136. Current research is indicating that a lot energy is lost by forced air heating and air-conditioning systems from air leaks throughout the duct system under your house or in the attic. That means the cooled or heated air does not really get to the places in your house where it is needed. You can accomplish a lot with a roll of duct tape and a little effort. Especially check for leaks at junctions and connections. Floor registers are another place were leaks are often found, even in new houses.

137. Even if you have central air conditioning, you might want to consider getting an auxiliary window unit to save energy. That way you can cool just one room, your bedroom for instance, so you can get a comfortable night's sleep, instead of cooling the whole house.

138. Ceiling fans should be at least 12" from the ceiling to be effective, ideally eight to nine feet from the floor, if the height of your ceilings permit it.

139. At the beginning of winter or the beginning of summer, it's always a good idea to check your fireplace damper to insure that it seals well so your fireplace is tightly closed off from outside air. Most fireplace dampers don't seal well and you can help with a bit of cleaning and adjusting.

140. To completely close off your chimney from outside air, consider an inflatable "chimney pillow" that will completely block off your fireplace, both sealing and insulating at the same time. Just remember to take it out before you build a fire.

141. Build a loft in your bedroom for sleeping comfort on those cold winter nights when you want to keep your heating costs down. Warm air rises and the loft will be considerably warmer than the room, so you can set your thermostat to a much cooler temperature.

142. Move your furniture as the seasons change. You don't want to sit near a window that lets in the sun in summer, but you do during winter. Keep your bed and chairs away from cold walls in the winter months.

143. If you have a window that lets in too much sun, try using ordinary aluminum foil on the outside to block the sun's rays. Leave an opening to let in some light, but you can block most of the light and heat from coming in with this simple solution. Use thumbtacks to hold it in place, as tape will quickly deteriorate.

144. If you don't have double pane windows, you can get much the same energy-saving effect by applying thermal

plastic coating. Be sure to replace the caulking anytime you see deterioration.

145. In cold weather use storm windows if you have them, get them up early in the season, and constantly check for leaks. If you live in an area where you don't have storm windows, check for drafts around all of your windows and doors.

146. If you have old windows or sliding doors that leak badly and are beyond weather-stripping or repairs, consider putting duct tape (it comes in colors) over the gaps around windows and doors during the coldest months. That means you can't open them during cold weather months, so be sure to leave at least two possible exits to every room in case there is a fire or other emergency.

147. In hot weather, open up windows from the top down to let out hot air and keep cool air in (hot air rises). If you have a two story house, open windows on the top floor to let hot air escape, or first open windows in the attic when it starts to get hot. That way the bottom half of the house stays cooler and you won't have to turn on the air conditioner quite as often.

148. Try to get your electric meter under control. Try turning off everything in the house, and then go and watch

the meter just as you did with your water meter. If it moves, go back in the house and unplug everything, and check your meter again. You will be shocked to find how difficult it is to get that thing to stop spinning. Then plug things back in one room at a time. This way you can discover where your biggest off-line energy drain is. You will be surprised where your energy is going; it's just like a leaky faucet! A little drain adds up over a long period of time. Be especially wary of those plug-in battery chargers like the one you have for your cell phone. Unplug, unplug, unplug when you aren't using them.

149. Re-caulk your windows and around bathroom fixtures whenever they become cracked. Most people think caulking around a bathtub is to keep water from getting under the floor, but it also serves to keep cold air from coming up from under the house. Most ceramic bathtubs sit directly on framing or rough flooring that is not sealed against the cold air under the house.

150. Use a stick of incense to find drafts around windows and doors, or you can slowly move the back of your hand around areas of potential leaks. This will help you find drafts and leaky windows in your house. Even new windows and doors can leak, so this applies to newer

houses as well. You can assume every window leaks until proven otherwise.

151. Check the weather stripping on all of your doors and windows. Add weather stripping and door seals wherever you find them worn or missing. This is a really low cost way to keep your house warmer in cold weather and cooler in summer. Weather stripping can be found in any good hardware store. You just peel off the backing and stick it on. Anyone can do it.

152. Buy "Energy Star" appliances. These devices meet or exceed standards set by the U.S. Department of Energy and the Environmental Protection Agency and can save you money year after year. You might want to trade your old appliances in early it if makes sense over the long term.

153. If you have to replace your roof or are remodeling or building a new home, look for energy efficient roofing. There can be a big difference in heat loss through the roof of your house. Some of the newer composite type roofing materials can dramatically add to the energy efficiency of your house.

154. A light colored roof reflects more sunlight and helps your house keep cooler in the hot summer months. If

your house has a dark colored roof, consider making it a lighter color. Yes, you can paint your roof! Check with your local roofing contractor or hardware store for products specific to this application.

155. Use your landscaping to save on energy bills--trees and shrubs can be used to shade your house from summer sun and to block cold winter winds.

156. Some power companies offer "energy plans" where your power is cut back during peak daytime hours when you are usually not home. The result is substantially lower energy bills. Ask your utility company for details.

157. Ask if your utility company will work with you to install solar panels on your roof and generate your own electricity. Or get a wind generator if you live in a windy area. Some utilities will even pay you for the energy you put back into the grid.

158. Use compact fluorescent bulbs wherever you can. Incandescent light bulbs run much warmer, and heat kills a bulb faster than anything. This is especially true for light bulbs in "cans" or enclosed fixtures. Cooler running fluorescent bulbs last longer, use less energy, and if fluorescent lighting bothers your eyes, know that

now you can find them in color temperature ranges that are similar to incandescent bulbs.

159. Use solar powered outdoor lights that can be found in most hardware and warehouse stores. They have batteries to store up energy during the day and come on automatically at night. Operating just one 100-watt bulb for 12 hours per night can add $40 to your annual utility bills

160. If you need a lot of light for security, low-pressure sodium (LPS) bulbs are the most efficient HID (High Intensity Discharge) lighting.

161. Everyone knows that Compact Fluorescent Lights (CFL's) save money, but did you also know that there are "high visual acuity" CFL's designed for reading? Check it out; there are many special-purpose CFLs that can save you money. Overall, CFL's use about 75% less electricity than standard incandescent bulbs.

162. When using a light for reading or close-up work, be sure that your eye can't see the bulb. When your eye detect a bright light it naturally closes the iris making it appear as if you need more light, and you'll reach for a higher wattage bulb than you need. To get the most efficiency

from task lighting, the light should be positioned above or behind your head.

163. Use fewer light bulbs by using higher wattage bulbs. It takes eight 25-watt light bulbs to make the same number of lumens as one 100-watt bulb. Higher wattage bulbs are more efficient at making light. Be sure not to use bulbs with wattage ratings that are higher than those suggested by the fixture manufacturer.

164. Light bulbs collect dust, and that reduces their efficiency by up to a third. While you are dusting the rest of the house, reach inside lamps and dust those bulbs. Clean bulbs last longer because there is less heat trapped inside the bulb.

165. If you use Christmas lights on your house, use the "midget" bulbs. The bigger bulbs use exponentially more electricity for the same effect.

166. Lighter colored walls and ceilings reflect more light, so you can get by with fewer bulbs to light a room. You might want to consider repainting dark rooms, or at least their ceilings.

167. Clean walls and ceilings reflect more light for the same reasons.

168. Lighter colored floors also reflect more light, but the savings may be offset by more frequent cleaning if your lifestyle demands it.

169. We all know it's not good for your eyes to watch TV with the lights off. What you want is low-wattage indirect lighting to "set the mood," and the good news is that this type of lighting uses much less energy than a lamp or bulb. Try to get a good balance between the brightness of your TV and the lighting in the room. You'll probably find you can use much less lighting than you're used to.

170. If you remember from the "old days" how fluorescent lights work, you may be leaving them on too long and for the wrong reasons. Today's fluorescent lights use modern, efficient ballasts, meaning you can turn them on and off just like incandescent bulbs without wasting energy. If you really want to get technical about it, limit use to 5 minutes. If you aren't going to use the light within the next five minutes, it's more energy-efficient to turn it off.

171. As light bulbs get older they lose their brilliance. Move older bulbs to areas where you don't need as much light, and keep newer bulbs where you want bright lighting.

172. Considering the astronomical prices of electricity, natural gas and oil, it's a good idea to check out alternative energy sources. Contact your local utility regarding the feasibility of solar panels or a wind powered generator for your property. Many times the utilities will actually pay you for the energy you put back into the "grid." You'll have to sharpen your pencil to see if this works for you, but with rising fuel costs, it is becoming more and more of a financially feasible option for many homeowners.

173. Use thermal plastic coating on windows that face north and east to help insulate against cold mornings.

174. Check the seal on your garage doors if your garage is attached to your house.

175. If you spend evenings in front of the TV, move the TV to cooler rooms of your house in summer, warmer rooms in winter, and adjust your thermostat accordingly to save energy year round.

176. Whenever you replace a heater or appliance, consider the energy sources available and work out the total energy cost for each energy source. The choices include electricity, oil, propane, LPG, natural gas, and solar.

Your local utility has experts who will help you with the calculations. Call them.

177. When you take a shower during humid weather, let the steam go outside by opening a window. You don't want to raise the humidity; it's cheaper to cool dry air.

178. If you use a window fan, only run it when there is at least a 20 degree difference between inside and outside temperatures, otherwise it's a waste of energy.

179. Get glass doors for your fireplace. They are energy efficient because they keep warm room air from going up the chimney, and at the same time, the glass still lets in the infra-red heat that actually warms you.

180. If you don't have glass doors on your fireplace (and maybe even if you do--you'll have to try it), crack a window closest to the fireplace to feed the draft from the fire. This helps to keep the warm air in the rest of your house from being drawn into the room and up the chimney.

181. If you have a fan in your bathroom, you will want to clean out that vent as well. It's not as important as your dryer vent, but getting humidity out of your house in hot weather saves the air conditioner, so you want to make sure your bathroom fan is venting effectively.

182. In extreme weather, make sure your windows are locked. Fastening the locks on windows often pushes them tighter against the weather stripping, thereby reducing the possibility of drafts.

183. You don't have to spend extra money on expensive remedies for "pet odors" in your carpet. Baking soda works just fine and costs much less. Just sprinkle some on the area, brush it in and vacuum.

184. Although snow feels cold on your hands and feet, it can actually be a good insulator and sealer for the foundation of your house. There is potentially a good deal of energy lost through the exposed foundation surface of most houses. There is also a lot of air leakage where the house walls rest on the top of the foundation. Caulk or seal from both sides for best results.

185. If you have an older color television with an "instant-on" feature, it is burning up energy when it is turned off. Especially if you don't watch it that often, unplug it when it's not in use.

186. Get your power company to do an energy audit of your home, office, and business. This service is almost always free and you can find ways to save money on energy you didn't even know about.

187. Keep track of your month to month usage of all of your utilities and compare to previous years. If there is a sudden increase in usage, look for a water leak or power drain and repair the cause.

188. Turn down the thermostat, turn off the water, take shorter showers, fix that dripping faucet, insulate your home, give your water heater a blanket, upgrade to energy efficient appliances... all of these things you hear about make a difference, especially over the long term. A big difference. Every dollar you save each year compounds into greater wealth in the future.

189. Extreme Utility Savings – go to bed early and rise with the sun, set your thermostat to 50 degrees in winter and bundle up instead of using a heater to keep warm, forget that you even own an air conditioner when it's hot, and all year 'round you can minimize all of your energy use by turning off lights, unplugging everything you aren't using, and washing everything (including you) less often.

Save Money on Homeowner's Insurance

190. Know what is covered and know what you are paying for insurance coverage. That means you have to break out the various types of homeowners coverage and break

down the cost for each. That way you can look for better rates from individual suppliers.

191. Buy specific coverage from providers who specialize. Earthquake coverage is often much cheaper at a specialty company. The same goes for flood insurance if you live in a "flood plain." For example, in California you will find the California Earthquake Authority (www.earthquakeauthority.com) for earthquake related information and insurance. FEMA can give you flood information - www.fema.gov.

192. Did you know "flood" is the most common cause of home disasters? The wild changes in our weather in recent years have meant that even homeowners in desert areas have experienced flood damage, and you can bet the majority of them didn't have flood insurance. Consider flood insurance even if you don't live in a typical flood area but know it could happen in extreme circumstances. You can get flood coverage information at FEMA - www.fema.gov.

193. If you live in a condo or belong to a homeowner's association, find out what kinds of insurance coverage they are already providing so you don't "double insure."

194. Just as with your car insurance, the higher your deductible the lower your costs, but check it out carefully because dollar-for-dollar your money buys significantly more coverage with your homeowner's insurance than your auto insurance. You might be giving up too much protection just to save a buck.

195. Shop around for the lowest rates but also be wary of the insurance company's financial strength and stability. These two web sites can give you that information: (www.ambest.com) and (www.standardandpoors.com). You want a company that is B+ or better.

196. Insure your house, not your land. No one can steal your land, or burn down your soil. Earthquake and flood insurance should take care of the things that could actually affect your land, so that's not the issue here. That means the amount of homeowner's insurance coverage you need in a worst case scenario needs to cover the value of the re-construction of your house only, along with other essential structures you would need to replace due to loss. Your insurance should cover the cost of rebuilding your home at today's costs, not what was paid to build it years ago.

197. Inventory the precious contents of your home with a video camera on a regular basis. Make copies of all of

your receipts and keep them with the most recent video tape someplace other than your home, such as your office or a safe deposit box. For the contents portion of your homeowner's insurance, set the value of the possessions you keep in your home at their replacement value, not what they are worth today (unless you are going to replace with equivalent "used" – and that's another way to save money if it works for you). Check with your insurance agent.

198. Strengthen your home and take action now to prevent potential disasters from affecting you later. Good planning can divert flood waters from damaging your home – culverts, berms, swales and good drainage systems are viable options. Strengthening the foundation and structure of your home, and especially any masonry fireplace chimneys, can greatly reduce the potential for damage in earthquake-prone areas. Think prevention!

199. Improve your home security buy installing deadbolts on all exterior doors, an alarm system that notifies a 24/7 service, trimming hedges and shrubs that block the view to vulnerable entry areas, and locking up carefully whenever you leave.

200. If you are thinking of moving and buying a new home, find out how much your homeowner's insurance is

going to cost you in the new neighborhood. Some areas are significantly higher than others, and it can sometimes change from one side of the street to the other depending on how the insurance companies draw the boundaries.

Save Money on Car Insurance

201. Control your insurance rates – a good driving record can save you tens of thousands of dollars in car insurance in your lifetime. Those dollars you save can be invested and turned into wealth - we're talkin' serious money here. Shop for the best rates at least once a year and avoid the trap of being "friendly" with your insurance agent. Get used to changing insurance carriers to always get the best rate year after year. Use a higher deductible. The difference between a $250 deductible and a $500 deductible can mean hundreds of dollars in savings on your insurance. And shop, shop, shop those rates!

202. When you shop for insurance, look for associations you can join that offer the same insurance at a substantial discount to its members. Trade and industry associations often offer great insurance deals to their members. Some membership/warehouse stores have insurance plans. Likewise shop for the best property, health and life insurance rates and do whatever you can to keep

those rates as low as possible. It's no secret that smokers pay far higher rates for insurance than non-smokers. If you are a senior citizen, make sure your car insurance company is giving you their "senior" discount.

203. Shop around for insurance every time you have to make another premium payment. You will be surprised how much you can save by looking for another quote every time you get a bill. Most people are hesitant to switch insurance companies so frequently, but the truth is it makes no difference how often you switch; you won't be turned down just because you switch often, and you will be assured of always getting the best rates.

204. Only deal with insurance companies with an "A" rating. To be safe, stick with nationally recognized insurers. No-name insurance companies who offer unbelievably cheap rates often have poor ratings and are no bargain if you ever have to file a claim or are involved in an accident. That's when you really get to pay for those "low-cost" premiums.

205. Your driving record is key to getting good insurance rates. Ask for a copy of your driving record from your local DMV to insure that there are no errors. Just like a credit report, errors can creep onto your driving record, and it's up to you to get them removed. Protect your

driving record and keep your insurance rates low with good driving habits, a "big rear-view mirror," and a good dose of common sense when you are driving. Remember, more people get speeding tickets than any other type of moving violation. If you are passing everyone else on the highway, sooner or later you are going to attract the attention of the local patrol. If someone wants to pass you, let them go by knowing that they are going to be the "rabbit" that gets caught in the trap, not you.

206. Always keep your registration and insurance certificate handy. If you do get stopped, be polite and answer questions honestly – that's absolutely the best way to "talk yourself out of a ticket." You'd be surprised how many people turn a ticket into a warning just by being polite, calm and honest during a traffic stop.

207. If your car is involved in a minor accident and yours is the only one damaged with no police report being filed, carefully consider if you want to file an insurance claim for repairs. Insurance companies raise your rates based not only on how many "points" you have on your driving record, but also by how many claims you have filed. This applies even if it wasn't your fault like when your car was the victim of a "hit-and-run" in a parking lot. If the repairs are only a few hundred dollars

over your deductible, consider paying it yourself out-of-pocket because you will pay many times that amount in increased insurance rates if you file a claim, especially if you already have "points" against your driver's license.

208. If you do have an accident and your insurance company is paying for collision repairs, don't ask the body shop to fix damage that was pre-existing by claiming it happened in the accident. For example, if you have accident damage to the front of your car and your windshield has been cracked for many months, don't try to get the insurance to pay for a new windshield by claiming it happened as part of the accident. You might get the insurance adjuster to pay for it now, but don't be surprised if it comes back to cost you many times over in the form of higher rate increases. Yes, they can do that! Body shops and insurance adjusters have seen it all; you aren't going to fool them.

209. Raise your deductible - for collision and comprehensive insurance from $500 to $1000 and you will save more than $500 in the next two years in most cases. That extra $500 in deductibles is an example of some of the most expensive insurance you will ever buy.

210. Gap Insurance: if your car is worth less than you owe, you are what is called "upside-down" in your loan. With

72 and 84 month vehicle loans, for the first three to five years there is almost a certainty you are upside down. Of course, we don't recommended borrowing to buy a vehicle, but some of you already have long term vehicle loans at zero or very low interest that you aren't going to pay down any time soon. The problem here is that if your car is totaled, your insurance will not pay off the balance due on your loan. Your insurance company check will only cover the current value of your vehicle based on age, condition, and miles driven. It is very possible that you will find yourself stuck holding a big balance due with no car to drive. When you buy gap insurance you are insuring more than your car, you are also protecting your credit. To avoid a "balance due" that you can't afford on a car you don't have, consider "gap insurance." You only need it for the period of time you are upside-down in your car loan. As a bonus, gap insurance usually pays your deductible as well, and that can be a big help when you have to buy another car. This insurance is relatively cheap - about $2 a month, at the most but we expect that to go up as people catch on.

211. Another insurance similar to this one is "diminished-value" insurance. For example, your car may have been repaired after a flood and returned to you in good driving condition, but the fact is "salvage" or "flood"

vehicle history is permanently noted on the title; and you will not be able to sell it for a retail used car price ever again. This loss of value is covered by diminished-value insurance and is highly recommended if you frequently park your car in a known flood zone.

212. Driving School – some insurance companies offer discounts for drivers under 25 who have been to an approved driving school. Good grades often result in a discount, so be sure your insurance company gets a copy of your child's transcript.

213. Should you buy an extended service contract on your car? In a word, No! Ask the dealer who wants to sell you one for three references of people who have bought such a contract, had a serious mechanical problem, and were happy with their extended guarantee. You won't get even one. When you file a "claim" there are so many exclusions and loopholes you will rarely get full payment for the cost of the repair.

Save Money on Vehicle Use and Maintenance

214. The average American family uses about 1500 gallons of fuel in a year. With the price of gas over $2.50 per gallon almost everywhere and approaching $3, $4 or even $5 a gallon in many places, that means we are

going to be spending over $3,000 to $7,000 a year just on fuel for our vehicles. A 10% savings is worth $300 to $700, and a 15% savings is worth $450 to $1050.

215. Most of us look for good prices on gas and diesel by watching the posted prices at our local stations, but did you know that prices go up just before the weekend? The best day to buy fuel is on Tuesday, never on those Saturdays when you are going out shopping or leaving on a weekend trip. If you plan ahead and buy your fuel earlier in the week you can save up to 10% every week - even more on big holiday weekends like Labor Day and Memorial Day.

216. Gas prices are volatile. As soon as you hear "bad news" that can affect oil prices or gasoline production, fill up your cars right away, before the price increase goes into effect. Remember, it's just as easy to keep the top half of your tank full as it is to keep the bottom half full. When you've got a full tank and there is a sharp price increase, you can wait it out to see if the price retreats after the "emergency" passes as it so often does.

217. You can save again by not driving around looking for more stations in your area with low fuel prices. There are at least two web sites that have fuel price comparisons: www.gaspricewatch.com and www.gasbuddy.com. By

checking with these web sites, you can plan your route and buy gas where it is cheapest without going out of your way. If you don't know where a particular station is, get the address by visiting www.mapquest.com for directions.

218. If you are going on a trip, use these web sites to plan your trip so you always get fuel where it is cheapest. You'll need to know how far your vehicle can go on a full tank, and then with www.GasBuddy.com or www.GasPrice.com you can plan your stops to get the best gas prices for the entire route of your trip. A good rule of thumb is to always keep the top half of your tank filled with lower priced gas. If you can't keep your tank full with cheaper gas, only fill the bottom half of the tank with more expensive fuel, and wait until you can get a better price to fill up to the top.

219. Always keep the tags on your vehicle up-to-date. You might not get stopped by the highway patrol, if you are lucky, but did you know that parking enforcement can cite you for expired tags? The worst are in airport parking lots where they can set the fine as high as they want.

220. Go a day without driving your car, then try to not drive two days a week, then three or four. See how far you

can go without driving. Ride a bike, ride the bus, bum a ride, whatever it takes. The bottom line: you must at least be able to give up driving one day a week. When you can do that every week, you'll cut your fuel expense by 14% a year, and that's a big savings. If you find you are unable to not drive for even one day, you need to change your lifestyle or you'll never be able to save real money on fuel costs.

221. Keep your car waxed and polished, use seat covers, floor mats and "detail" the interior on a regular basis. Never smoke in your car. Keep a clear journal of service and repairs, along with all the receipts. When it's time to sell your used car, these measures can add thousands to the price you will get from a private party sale.

222. If you live near the ocean or where there is exposure to salt, put wax on the chrome parts of your car just like you would on the paint. It will help prevent pitting and rust. You'll have to use a chrome polish first before you wax. Do this simple task whenever you wax your car and your chrome will last much longer, and it will help to hold up the resale value of your car.

223. When your car battery dies it's usually been very hard on the alternator, because the alternator has been having to constantly make up for the ability to hold a charge

the battery has lost. It doesn't happen overnight, it takes weeks or months for a battery to "die." Have your alternator checked out thoroughly whenever you replace a battery. A bad or weak alternator will wreak havoc on the entire electrical system, especially computers and engine systems, not to mention the starter and the battery.

224. If your battery goes dead because you left the lights on or a door open, it is much better to use a battery charger to recharge the battery. Avoid using jumper cables on modern cars! Should you accidentally cross the polarity, you can fry every computer and electronic system in your vehicle. Even if you are successful at getting it started with jumper cables, driving the vehicle with a run down battery puts a tremendous load on all the systems.

225. If you have a high-profile car that thieves love, keep it in the garage and whenever you can, park it where it's safe.

226. A flashing red LED light inside your car can fool thieves into thinking you have an active alarm system. LED's are cheap and easy to install. Check your local electronics (Radio Shack) or car parts, car stereo/alarm store for supplies.

227. Use a steering wheel lock to deter car theft. It's clumsy, but it's the most effective car theft prevention device known to man.

228. A hidden "cut off" switch that disables the ignition or fuel pump is also very effective.

229. When driving your car up a long hill, let up on the gas just before you crest the top. This will keep you from picking up speed on the downhill side and saves fuel.

230. Slowing down early when you see a stop sign or red light ahead saves fuel and brakes. Don't run right up to a red light and slam on your brakes at the last minute just because you were hoping it would turn to green. The odds are against you getting it right. Smooth driving is a skill that saves fuel. The most fuel is used in getting a vehicle moving from a dead stop; a "rolling stop" uses much less fuel. But don't break the law doing it! You still have to come to a full stop at stop signs.

231. Car keys have become very complex with integrated electronics for theft deterrence. If you lose them, it can be quite expensive to get replacements. For that reason, always put your keys in the same exact place every time you walk in the door, change your clothes, or arrive at the office. Train yourself consciously to do

this for 30 days and it will become a habit. Life is easier when everything has its place, and you'll help avoid the unnecessary expense of replacing your keys.

232. Never leave your keys in the car. Never warm your car up in the driveway. Thieves look for telltale exhaust vapor during the morning go-to-work hours, especially in the suburbs.

Save Money on Education

233. Move to an area with good public schools for your children and forego the unbelievably high expense of a private school. 12 years x $7,000 a year (about the national average) is $84,000 for each child before they even get to college… and that doesn't even calculate the interest and compounding you'd get on those dollars-- the potential "savings" is approximately $200,000 per child or more!

234. When saving for college, check out the tax free savings plans that are available. What you are looking for is called a qualified tuition program (QTP) that allows you to put away pre-tax dollars for future education. Check it out at http://www.irs.gov/pub/irs-pdf/p970.pdf.

235. Buy used textbooks. Everyone knows this, but sometimes you can't find the used textbook you need at the campus

books store. As a cost-saving solution, first find out the used book prices at the student bookstore and then look for an even better deal at online sources. There are many online web sites where you can buy used books instead of paying new prices at the book store. And their prices for new books are often cheaper too, even after shipping charges. Simply go to www.google.com and type "used textbooks" into the search window. You will see hundreds, if not thousands, of sources.

236. Share books with a friend. In many upper class curricula at colleges and universities, the professor will require "supplemental" books and textbooks that are used infrequently (if ever!). Find a friend who will go in with you and share these kinds of books and half the expense.

237. When you go to college it's best to leave your car at home, but if you just have to have a car, don't buy a parking permit from your college or university; they are just too expensive. If at all possible, do your parking off campus and walk the rest of the way. You will want to buy several one-day passes for those occasions when you just *have to* park on campus (being late for an exam comes to mind), but it's still much cheaper than a full time permit.

238. If you live in a dorm but come home on weekends, bring your dirty laundry with you. Coin-operated laundry machines are money bandits, and they are hard on your clothes too.

239. Never use on-campus vending machines for quickie meals. Buy snacks ahead of time and carry them in your backpack. Why pay two or three times as much for the same thing out of a vending machine?

240. The biggest waste of money for any college student is eating out. Even if you live in a dorm room, you can still prepare meals "at home" and avoid the huge expense of eating around or off-campus. Make a salad, sandwich or a bowl of instant soup for lunch or dinner, and never pay cafeteria prices again.

241. If your student isn't accomplished at discount shopping and savings, chances are a roommate or fellow student is. Tell your student to seek these people out and become savings partners with them; adopt their mindset and find out how they do it. You will be amazed at how little money some people get by on, and you'd never know the difference in the way they live. It can be the best "education" they will get.

242. Enroll your fellow students in a "group savings plan." Let's face it, it's not too hard to find other students who are hard pressed for cash, and most of them don't know how to shop and save. When students work together as a group they can share discounts on bulk items, coupons, special offers, lowest prices, sales and any "deals" they find. Comparison shopping, coupon clipping and bargain hunting take a lot of time and effort, but when several like-minded people work together to save money, all sorts of great ideas and savings can result.

243. Always ask local stores if they have a "student discount." Even if you don't see it in print or in their advertisements, most will give you a discount if you ask for it. Offer to spread the word around campus for the store if they will start a student discount program.

244. Take advantage of any of the free or low-cost services offered by the college or university. Low cost medical and dental care is offered at many colleges and universities, and some services are free. For example, watch for free health screening at "Health Fairs" and get free check-ups and diagnostic tests. Even parents and siblings can get in on the act if they live nearby, as these events are open to the public but not usually advertised publicly.

245. Most colleges and universities have free job-search programs, and they have trained counselors that are available to help with employment issues. You can use these services even years after you graduate, although most people don't think to do it. Why would you pay a job counselor or head hunter to do what your alma mater does better and for free?

246. Most college libraries offer free internet access and there are tons of newspapers and magazines available, usually many more than at a public library, so you never have an excuse to buy a subscription again. This is a great tip even if you aren't a college student--if you live near a college or university, you'll find, in most cases, the university library is open to the public and offers many services you won't find in any public library.

247. Scholarships take work and you have to continually seek out scholarship application opportunities, but no job you could ever get pays what you will receive from scholarships for the few hours of work it takes to apply for them. Each year hundreds of millions of scholarship dollars go undistributed because of lazy students, otherwise deserving, who don't take the time to apply. Make scholarship application Job #1!

Save Money on Medical Expenses

248. Vitamins and supplements are seductive in their promises, but they are destructive to your pocketbook, especially since most have no real health benefit. Chances are most of the vitamins and minerals you are taking as supplements are already present in sufficient quantity in your diet, and all you are doing is making "expensive urine." The body only absorbs about 15% of the vitamins you take in a supplement under even the best of conditions. Natural foods are the best source of vitamins and minerals. Consult with a good nutritionist (look for a free clinic!) and stop wasting money on vitamins and supplements that do no body good.

249. If you don't have health care insurance and need to go to a doctor, ask the doctor for a break. Explain your situation and if you have good reasons (kids in college, lost your job, etc), you will find that many times the doctor will bill you for a less expensive procedure than what you actually received. Yes, even a doctor's care is negotiable. And be sure to ask at the front desk if they offer a cash discount.

250. Ask for "samples" of the prescription the doctor is recommending for you. Most doctors have tons of prescription samples they'll give you if you ask, and

this can ultimately save money on your prescriptions. If you have an ongoing problem, be sure to ask for more samples at each visit and make your Rx go further between refills.

251. Find the right kind of doctor for your health. If you have a problem with your teeth, you wouldn't first make an appointment with a family physician to get a referral to a dentist would you? But most people don't realize that if that you have a specific health concern you can go straight to a specialist and avoid the unnecessary expense of seeing a family physician for a referral. This is especially true for men's and women's health issues. Talk to people you know with similar health problems and listen to their story. Usually you will hear the words, "… finally I went to doctor so-and so and she knew what was wrong with me…" It can save you time and money while getting you the care you need faster by going right to the specialist.

252. Always get a second opinion where there is a major medical expense involved. Too many times the diagnosis is incorrect or incomplete, or the recommended treatment is inappropriate. It makes no sense to incur a big medical expense for a problem you didn't have

in the first place! Always, always, always get a second opinion.

253. Quite often the problem can be treated just as effectively with less expensive alternatives. It makes dollars and sense to thoroughly educate yourself about the disease, symptoms and treatments, and become your own best medical advisor, working in cooperation with your doctor. Many problems can be more effectively treated when you make appropriate changes in diet and lifestyle, and that saves you a ton of money.

254. Get treated early when you know you have a problem. The longer you wait to get diagnosis and treatment, the more expensive the cure. Most common problems, high blood pressure for example, can be handled quickly and easily with today's medications and modern therapies, but when they are ignored or neglected it can turn into a major medical problem that can strip you of your life savings. It's another reason to keep looking for those free diagnostic clinics! And this is a great example of where changes in diet and lifestyle can save you significant amounts of money you'd otherwise pay for medical bills.

255. If you know something is bad for you, stop doing it! If you have a vice like cigarettes, coffee, overeating, drugs

or alcohol, you are wasting your money and robbing yourself of your future health. Put that same money you spend on 'vices' in a piggy bank and you will be shocked at how much is in there at the end of just one year.

256. If you have been diagnosed with a chronic health condition, contact local medical universities and ask the medical schools if there are any clinical studies that would be interested in your case. Some clinical studies will even pay you a stipend to participate, and you will almost always receive free medical treatment and checkups for your troubles. Try www.clinicaltrials.gov for a listing of clinical trials in your area.

257. Make your own skin care products. Many of the expensive facial crèmes and other types of skin care products are nothing more than new combinations of stuff that's been around forever. Read the ingredients on the label and then go to a natural health food store, buy the same ingredients, and make your own. You will save tons of money, and you may discover that the perfect combination for your skin doesn't come from a pre-mixed commercial product.

258. Exercise is good for you, and a health club is a great place to get it. But when a pair of sneakers and the open

road offer the same benefits, why pay more? Need an instructor to lead you? Get a video tape from the public library and put the membership fee in your savings account. Invite some friends over and have an exercise party.

259. Find friends with similar health problems (overweight anyone?) and work together to improve your health. Walking, jogging and/or exercising regularly with a friend will keep you on track, and you won't need the expense of a health club to do it.

260. Same goes for dieting. It's all about support and accountability to each other, and you don't need to pay someone for that. Ask a friend, ask a relative, and get it together.

261. Check out the YMCA for exercise and swimming classes that are very low cost or sometimes free. Be sure to watch for special offers and free introductory periods at the "Y" and local gyms.

262. Look in the calendar section of your newspaper for free cooking and health classes offered at local clinics, schools and public institutions that will help you on your way to better health.

263. Nothing is more devastating to your wealth than a health crisis. You know the basics; a good diet and a healthy lifestyle that includes exercise along with good stress reduction strategies such as regular rest and some recreational fun are essential to your health.

264. Look for discount pharmacies when you need to get a prescription filled. Some medications are available through the internet at huge discounts. Take advantage if your company offers flexible spending accounts for medical expenses. With these types of accounts you can pay for prescriptions and medical services with pre-tax dollars. Look for alternatives to traditional medical care. Always get a second or third opinion before any medical or dental procedure: a significant percentage of invasive therapies such as surgeries are later found to have been unnecessary and sometimes harmful to the patient's health.

265. When you take good care of your health you are more productive and happier in your job, can work longer and better, and have fewer missed days from work-- all of which can ultimately affect your career and your wealth.

266. Good health means that you and your family are not burdened with the expenses, inconvenience and loss

of quality of life that are associated with disease and disability. After all, there is no point in becoming wealthy if you aren't going to be healthy enough to enjoy it.

Save Money at the "Home Office"

267. A home office is great because you don't have to drive to work, and that saves you tons of money right there. The key is to keep "office expenses" under control by shopping around for all of your supplies and services.

268. If you are starting a business, get advice from retired business owners. Many communities have resources where you can get the advice of retired business executives for free. Check with your local Chamber of Commerce for leads.

269. When you are just setting up, look for used or auction items for desks, chairs, equipment and fixtures. It's amusing how when a business is starting out they have to buy everything new, and when they go out of business no one wants their stuff. This is one area where you can save a ton of money. TIP: call around to office managers and landlords who have tenants moving out and tell them about your needs. Offer to haul away for free anything the tenants leave behind. They will even thank you for

it! If they try to charge you, negotiate a very, very low price. They really don't want to deal with it.

270. If that doesn't work, try your local recycling centers. Many waste disposal sites have "last chance" outlets for perfectly good office furniture that someone was in a hurry to dump--probably someone like that property manager you just talked to.

271. Used computers are great bargains for the home office. A word processor, or a database or spreadsheet requires very little computing horsepower. If your business needs are modest, you can do very well with a computer that is 2-3 years old, and you should have to pay no more than $100 to $150 to get a serviceable unit.

272. Need a website? Don't call a web master or internet genius, do it yourself. Almost anyone who can run a word processor can set up an internet site on one of the pre-packaged deals that abound on the internet today. Try www.citymax.com for starters and go from there. Or search google.com for "web site templates" if you are into the "do-it-yourself" idea but you really want a more "custom" look.

273. Do you really need a high speed internet connection? Probably not if you are like most home office users.

Email and messaging are easily handled with a modem connection through your existing phone line and you will save at least $300-$400 a year. Don't get a high speed connection unless you absolutely need it. "Cruising" the internet can be a high speed diversion and an even quicker drain on your time and pocketbook. You want to make money, not spend it!

274. Refill your own ink cartridges. Manufacturers practically give away printers because they steal you blind by charging 10 times more for ink than what it costs to do it yourself. There are hundreds of do-it-yourself ink refill products on the internet. Try inputting "ink cartridge refill kit" on www.google.com and you'll get the idea. Before you buy a printer, make sure you can get a "refill kit" for that specific model. If you don't like the idea of ink refills, check to see if generic cartridges are available for your specific model at half or one-third of the manufacturer's discounted price. The manufacturers will try to tell you otherwise, but for home office use, ink is all the same (unless you are a graphics designer, but then if you were a graphic designer you'd already know that!).

275. Never buy an all-in-one printer/fax/copier. If one part breaks, you get to buy the whole thing over again, and

they are significantly more expensive than a "stand alone" printer. Besides, as we are about to tell you in #278 below, you really don't need a fax machine, and if you do need a scanner to make copies and capture images, it's still cheaper to buy a scanner and a printer than an all-in-one for the same resolution. The "PS" here is "don't buy a USED printer." It's just not worth it when new ones are dirt cheap.

276. Make high volume copies at a copy center like Kinko's - it's cheaper by far than using your home office computer and printer. If you need more than 50 or 100 copies, you should do at a center.

277. Recycle your own paper. In a home office you don't need to worry about appearances and you can use the back side of letters and documents instead of wasting fresh paper on drafts and other "in-house" printing you aren't sending to anyone.

278. Don't buy a fax machine; use an on-line fax service like www.efax.com. A fax machine has "consumables" just like a printer does; it takes up space, wastes paper, jams frequently, and it's noisy. Why bother when you can receive paperless faxes through your email account and send them right from your word processor? It's just like printing a document except that it sends a fax instead.

Try punching "internet fax" into www.google.com for more ideas.

279. Sending packages to your customers? Check out the post office! It's now the most efficient branch of the US Government. Really! Try out their new "express mail" boxes where it's the same low price regardless of what it weighs. As long as it fits in the box, the price is the same and it's cheap and fast. The delivery is just as good as UPS (or better!), and the cost is half as much, or even lower now that UPS has gone "Brown." (Yuk, what marketing genius thought of that one?) Stick with the good ole Red, White, and Blue USPS and you won't regret it.

280. If you need a business loan, shop around and be sure to negotiate for the best rate. The first rate you are offered is never the lowest you can get, but you'll have to work at it. Ask, "What would I have to do to get a lower rate?" It may be as simple as keeping a little higher balance in your account, or paying off a loan.

281. If you are making payments on a loan, check to see if you can set up an automatic payment plan directly from your checking account at a preset date each month. Many lenders will give you an interest rate discount

if you do this. You'll save on the price of a stamp and never have a late fee. It's worth it!

282. If you work and put your kids in daycare, be sure to keep good records of the expense so you can take the child care credit at tax time. Check with your tax accountant for details on what records you will need.

283. You can pay your parents for childcare and as long as the cost is reasonable, and it's tax deductible.

284. If you love to spend money, then focus on spending money to make money. And we don't mean you should go on one of those "the more you spend the more you save" shopping sprees. We mean you need to focus on spending money on investments! You know, that's when you buy things that have a positive cash flow or an actual ROI (Return on Investment), like income property, certificates of deposit, savings accounts, notes, stocks and bonds.

285. If you keep valuables in a safe deposit box at the bank, you'll need to get insurance for those items. Banks don't insure the contents of safe deposit boxes whether damage or loss is from fire, theft or "acts of nature."

286. If you buy mutual funds, stick with "index" funds rather than "managed" funds. Mutual fund managers

historically have a terrible track record and seldom if ever can beat an index fund. Compare for yourself and save your dollars!

287. Single family homes don't make good "income property." Yes, there is more appreciation potential, but it's more important to focus on a positive cash flow, and a decent ROI from rental income. Check it out and you'll discover you only get that with rental units in multiple family dwellings.

288. Go to free investment seminars but don't buy anything. You'll get tons of great ideas and even some good advice for free. Save the money you would have spent on books, newsletters, and computer programs for your investments. If you are really interested in a newsletter, you will most likely find it at a college or university business school library where you can read it for free.

289. If you know you are going to owe the IRS a tax payment, file your return as late as possible. If you are owed a refund, file your return as soon as possible.

290. Look for ways your employer can help you reduce expenses. Get them to start a company car pool, supply coffee and snacks in the office for coffee breaks, offer stress reduction therapy such as massage or counseling,

give you a company car, install a company gas station where all employees can buy fuel at a discount, offer in-plant child care… the only limit is your imagination and your ability to ask, ask, ask.

291. Ask your employer if you can work at home one or more days a week. With the advent of internet and a laptop or home computer, it's easy to do the same amount of work without the expense of commuting to the office.

292. When your business grows, sub-contract work that requires an investment in machinery or equipment until you've made enough to justify the expense and you've had time to prove the market. You should consider renting instead of buying in the same circumstance.

293. Become active in your community doing volunteer work. You will meet all sorts of people you can network with to save money. Depending on the kind of work you are doing, you may find savings in the form of special discounts for volunteers, or even financial reimbursements for your expenses may be available to you. You may be able to take a tax deduction for expenses while doing charity work, so keep good records for tax time.

294. Never donate property that has declined in value. It has more value to you as a tax write-off. If you give a charity something that has appreciated in value, you not only get the tax credit, you save tax you would have had to pay on the capital gain.

295. Write off your expenses. Every dollar you pay in taxes is a dollar you didn't save, and it's lost to you forever. Americans lose millions and millions of dollars in missed tax deductions every year. Keep track of all of your deductible expenses and turn those tax dollars into savings dollars. If you don't itemize your expenses, it's time to find out how to do it. Hire a professional to help you the first year and be sure to always keep receipts and payment records for everything you buy.

296. If you think you need a pickup or van, think again. These vehicles are available for rental. Figure out how many days you really need to use these types of vehicles and then weigh the cost of ownership against the cost of rental. Your everyday car should be economical, and will be sufficient for ordinary use. On those rare occasions when you need a special use vehicle, rent one.

Save Money On Home Maintenance And Repairs

297. Mold and mildew can be a real problem in cold, damp climates. If you are repainting, use only special mold and mildew resistant paints and you'll save money by not having to repaint as often.

298. At the beginning of barbeque season, clean out the burners and venturi tubes if you use a gas unit. Spiders, bugs, and even frogs and lizards can make their winter home in your barbeque.

299. A ridge vent is another great idea for homes with attics. A ridge vent lets hot air escape from the upper area of the attic. Again, a cooler attic reduces air conditioning expense.

300. Where is the thermostat located in your house? You may want to relocate the thermostat from a hallway or wherever it is to someplace closer to where you spend most of your time, like the bedroom. It doesn't help much if the hallway or the inside of a closet is a comfortable temperature and where you are is unpleasantly warm or cold. Trying to compensate for the difference in location never seems to work out well. It's easier to just relocate the thermostat.

301. Old style thermostats have a bi-metal strip shaped like a coiled spring and a tube of mercury under the cover. This kind of mechanism is vulnerable to dust and dirt buildup. Pull the cover off and gently blow out the dust. Use a soft brush only if necessary. If a spider has made a home there, you will want to remove it and its web.

302. If you need to replace the windows in your house, casement windows are the most energy efficient. Reason: they seal better, have fewer gaps to leak air, and when they are open they work like an airfoil to help draw air into the house.

303. Window screens block the sun's rays. Use them to your advantage in summer to help shade your windows, but take them off in winter when you want the heat to come in.

304. Clean out "weep holes" in your windows before the storm season approaches to prevent water buildup in the casement during heavy rains.

305. Clean frames and sliders so weather stripping can get a good seal. Place a dollar bill under the seals and try to pull it out when the window is closed and locked. If you find a loose area, you may need to either adjust the window or replace the seals.

306. Lubricate window tracks and seals with silicon or WD40 for longer life and easier operation. Be sure to wipe off any excess that would attract debris.

307. Window screens will block some of the direct force of the winter winds, so leave them on the north- and east-facing windows.

308. If you use window screens, take them off south-facing windows in winter to let in more solar energy. Keep them on north windows to help block wind and cold.

309. If a window doesn't have to be open, it should always be locked. A locked window not only offers increased security, the weather stripping will also seal better because the lock presses the window tightly against the frame.

310. Replacing cracked window glass is more than just a safety item. Even if the crack looks small and insignificant, it will still leak cold air, especially if the wind is blowing. If you get a big storm, a cracked window will break more easily and could present a hazard with flying glass.

311. If you use solar panels to heat your swimming pool water or your home, or even to generate electricity, they need to constantly be adjusted to most directly face the sun as the seasons change. Most are set at an average

for the year, but you can gain efficiency by making seasonal adjustments. Check with the manufacturer for the optimal setting for your latitude at different times of the year.

312. Soffit vents allow cool air to be drawn into the attic and are found under the roof overhang. If your roof doesn't have them, adding soffit vents to your roof will lower your air conditioning bills significantly.

313. Debris on your roof can hold in heat during summer, keep in cold and damp in winter. Debris can collect around skylights, and in the worst case, can rot the wood on your roof.

314. When you replace your roof, use "lifetime" materials which are impervious to debris, such as ceramic, tile, or metal roofing. These materials are also incredibly fire proof.

315. Keep your gutters clean so water doesn't back up and rot your roof, or worse yet, rot the eaves underneath.

316. The roof of your house "radiates" infra-red heat on hot summer days. If you've ever been in your attic on a hot sunny day, you know what this feels like. You can reflect this infra-red heat back out of your house by stapling reinforced aluminum foil to the roof rafters. Not only

that, it will help keep heat inside your house in the winter.

317. If the roof of your house collects leaves and debris, you'll have to get up there and remove it. Debris holds humidity that rots your roof causing leaks and other problems.

318. Use a Class A roof to lower insurance costs because of its fire resistance and lifetime guarantee. It should never wear out or need replacement. If you are planning on living in your home for a long time, like maybe the rest of your life, it's a good investment.

319. Paint and caulk usually have a good shelf life, but if they are subjected to freezing temperatures they will be ruined and unusable. Be sure to store paints, caulks, glues, and sealers in an area that won't get below freezing in winter.

320. If the temperature is going to be below freezing at night, remove all your garden hoses from their hose bibs or faucets. In the morning, if you see an icicle, you will know you've got a leak that needs fixing, and you will have just saved your hose from being split open and ruined.

321. Avoid purchasing gas powered mowers, blowers, and trimmers. Buy electric models instead and you'll save hundreds of dollars every year in fuel and maintenance costs.

322. Keep a bucket in your shower to catch the first cold water stream and use it later to water your plants.

323. Measure how much you water plants and trees by filling a bucket or watering can. If you just let the water run for random amounts of time, you'll be wasting a lot of water. Dig basins around all of your plants and trees so the water soaks into the roots where you want it to and doesn't run off.

324. To most efficiently water your garden and lawn on hot summer days, use a soaker hose. Too much water is lost to evaporation with a sprinkler system.

325. Many plants don't like to have their leaves get wet, especially roses. Water only the ground around the base of plants and keep the leaves dry. Better yet, use a drip system on a regulated timer.

326. If you have decks around your home, take good care of them by regularly using a good finish and sealer – they will last two to three times as long, giving you a cost savings much greater than the relatively small expense

of a semi-annual refinish or touch up. Use a pressure washer before putting treatment on your deck for best results. The same goes for any wood stairs, railings, sashes, or other exposed wood.

327. The most important part of your air conditioner is the condenser coils. Whether it's a free-standing unit or a window unit, you'll have to remove the shroud to get at the condenser coils. They need a good cleaning at the beginning of the warm season. If you live in an area with a lot of humidity, you should check them every six weeks to two months.

328. Make sure the shroud goes back on securely and in the proper location, as the shroud is vital to good air circulation around the coils. Replace any missing screws and repair the shroud wherever it is bent or damaged.

329. Second most important is the air filter in your HVAC system. It doesn't do any good to have an efficient A/C condenser if the air can't circulate inside the house. Don't scrimp and buy the cheapo 99 cent filters; get the better quality filters. They will keep your house and your HVAC system cleaner.

330. Even window air conditioners need to be serviced and cleaned. Don't let their small size and portability distract

you from the need for annual cleaning for maximum efficiency.

331. When your air conditioner is running you should see water running out of the drain tube from the condenser. If not, the drain and drain tube are in need of cleaning. When water is trapped in the condenser it finds its way back into the air in your house, making it feel muggy.

332. Check all the duct work of your HVAC system for tightness and leakage at least once a season. If your basement or HVAC closet is warmer than your house., it's a sure fire tip off that you have a leak.

333. If you feel any vibration or unusual noises when your HVAC system is running, you've got a problem; check it out. Prompt attention to HVAC problems is always a very good idea.

334. Even new HVAC duct work can leak at the joints and corners. Both new and old HVAC sheet metal work can be less than leak proof. The solution is to buy a roll of duct tape and wrap every joint and corner you can find – just assume even if it looks new and tight, that it probably leaks anyway.

335. If you have central air conditioning, make sure the coolant lines that carry the refrigerant in and out of

your house are well insulated. These can be small copper tubes that you will see running from the air conditioning unit outside to someplace under your house where the "evaporator" for the HVAC is located. If you can see copper tubes, they're not insulated, and they should be for greater energy efficiency. Check for cracks in the insulation or missing sections along the whole length of the run and repair or replace where needed.

336. Put out to dry those "used" paper towels so you can use them again.

337. Use a bucket to catch the wash/rinse water from your laundry and use it to clean your car, floors, deck. It's free soapy water with lots of scrubbing power left in it.

338. Use lemon juice and baking soda instead of kitchen cleansers to clean the sink and counters in your kitchen.

339. Use baking soda and white wine vinegar as a drain cleaner. The chemical action of the two together will loosen and remove the gunk in most kitchen drains.

340. Never put coffee grounds down the drain or in your garbage disposal. The oils in coffee and the texture of the grounds tend to clog things up in the worst way.

By the way, coffee grounds work well in compost for the garden.

341. Check your garage door seal. If your garage is connected to your house in any way, a leaking seal under the garage door can cost you money.

342. When you upgrade your furnace, compare prices of different fuels. Natural gas is usually cheapest, but this can vary depending on where you live.

343. Put a bucket to catch the water in the shower while you wait for the temperature to come up. Use the water for plants.

344. After a bath, recover some of the water in a bucket and use the soapy water to wash your floors, car, patio and sidewalk.

345. Or use it to wash your pets.

346. Check the insulation in your attic each season. Make sure it is evenly distributed. In rainy weather, go up and check for damp insulation. Take it out when it gets wet and replace it after you fix the leak. Damp insulation is worse than no insulation.

347. Check the spaces around electrical conduit, pipes and plumbing where they enter or exit your house. Fill any

gaps with caulk or sealer. Be sure to check those hose bibs that come out of walls.

348. Ceiling fixtures such as lamps and fans may have hidden gaps where they mount that can leak air to the attic. Pull off the shade and take a look around the base of the lamp fixture. Caulk or fill any gaps to keep air from escaping into the attic.

349. Attic doors are often not sealed or insulated. Just as with any door, weather stripping helps keep air where it belongs. Insulation on the door itself helps too.

350. If you don't want the expense of a security system, put up the signage anyway. You could even go so far as to put a box and alarm bell on a wall where it's clearly visible. Thieves always go for what they think is the easy job, and these simple precautions could turn them away without the expense of a full system.

351. If the slab or foundation of your house has an exposed south face, take precautions to keep the sun off in summer and the cold off in winter. A planter box, deck, or berm will do the job nicely.

352. Refinish old ceramic sinks and bathtubs instead of replacing them. Not only do you save the cost of a new sink or tub, you save all the problems and expense

of installation in one of the most expensive repair areas in your home.

353. Blame the faucet if you have to constantly replace the washer to stop leaks. An old faucet that has a corroded seat will "eat" washers as fast as you can replace them. It's time for a new faucet if you are going to permanently stop that leak.

354. If you have a skylight, you've probably noticed a draft in really cold weather. You can install a magnetic window made of Plexiglas (acrylic) that will adhere to the bottom of the frame. Now you have not only stopped the draft, you've created an insulating barrier of air between you and the skylight.

355. If your skylight leaks water, that means it leaks air as well. Get up on your roof and check all the seals and replace and renew where needed. The same applies if you see spiders or insects entering your house through the skylight. There's an opening somewhere.

356. If you have a basement, you have a band joist. That's the part of the frame that rests on the foundation. In almost every home built in the last century, you'll find there is no insulation in this area. Seal all the cracks and

cover the band joist with insulating material and you will save on your heating and cooling bills

357. You can renew older kitchen brushes by washing them in the dishwasher; just be sure to remove them before the heat/drying cycle or they might melt!

358. Kitchen drains can clog up frequently, and a little prevention goes a long way. Never put coffee grounds down the drain, as they are oily and clog in cold water, even if you run them through the disposal. The same applies to fats and grease. It's much better to put these items in an old can with a lid on it and then into the trash.

359. Use of chemical drain cleaners are not advised in kitchen drains and should be avoided. You just don't want any chance of those kinds of substances coming into contact with any cooking surfaces or utensils. Instead, use a half cup of baking soda, followed by a half cup of vinegar. These two substances react in much the same way a drain cleaner works and will help to keep your drain smelling fresh too.

360. A lemon rind run through your garbage disposal at the end of your kitchen clean up leaves a fresh smell in your kitchen and helps break down grease in the drain.

361. To check the seals on the weather stripping around your doors, use a dollar bill. Close the door and the dollar bill should stick in the jamb. If it's loose, you've got a weak or bad seal that needs to be checked. Or you may need to adjust the striker plate so the door closes more tightly.

362. When you plant shrubs and bushes close to your house, try to use varieties with thorns or stickers under and around windows or other areas that could be favored by a thief or burglar. You might just save yourself the cost of a break-in.

363. Motion-sensing lights are more effective in deterring thieves than flood lights because of the "surprise" element. Look for solar powered, self-contained units. They are more cost efficient and environmentally friendly. Another real advantage is that you can mount them anywhere without having to run wires, meaning you can put them where they will do the most good.

364. Set motion-sensing lights to stay on for no more than 5 minutes after a motion is detected. That way you won't have pesky nocturnal animals like possums and skunks or the family cat running up your light bills or running down the batteries in your solar powered units.

365. Hire a chimney sweep (or do it yourself) at least once a season if you use your fireplace during the winter months. Not only will your fireplace be more efficient and give you more heat, there is a risk of an uncontrolled fire when too much soot builds up in the chimney and dampers.

366. The room outlets for your HVAC system are called "registers." If you notice that the air coming out of the registers is not going where you want it to, you can find clear plastic "diverters" at the hardware store that will allow you to direct the air flow where you want it, making your system more efficient.

367. To keep your home warmer in winter months, think like the wind. When that cold wind blows, where does it come from, what direction? Take measures to block cold air coming down against your house and seeping inside. Cold air flows down hill. Use a hedge, trees, berms, or even strategically placed out-buildings to block the cold winds of winter.

368. Cold air moves downward; for example, it's always coldest down in a valley compared to up on a protected hillside. If you have a choice of where to build, always pick the high ground. Avoid building where cold air gravitates on a cold night.

369. If you live where winters are brutally cold, be careful not to plant trees and shrubs where they could block the southern exposure, and therefore warming sunlight.

370. Similarly, the north side of a valley gets more sun in winter and shade in summer than the south side of an east-west valley. If you are building, pick a site that is inherently energy efficient.

371. If you don't have mature trees to block the hot sun in summer, use awnings and curtains to shade the inside of your house from the sun. Window screens can help too.

372. One use for old newspapers is as mulch in the garden. They keep weeds down and hold in moisture. By the end of the season they will be crumbling, and you can turn them into the soil with the rest of your garden. Use only black ink newspapers, avoid color or glossy pages. Most black ink is soy based, while color comes from often-toxic chemicals and dyes you don't want in your garden soil. Use old newspapers to clean windows – it saves on paper towels.

373. Some "weeds" are good for gardens. Dandelions, for example, are favored by many varieties of birds, and you want to invite birds into your garden to eat the bugs.

Just don't let the dandelions go to seed or you'll have thousands of them everywhere.

374. If you feed the birds, they will return the favor by eating more of the bugs in your garden. The more birds you attract, the fewer bugs you will find.

375. If you have a problem with snails and slugs in your garden, encourage possums to come into your yard by leaving out dry dog or cat food overnight. Once there, they will quickly clean out your garden of the slimy pests and do little harm to your plants. Make sure your dog is inside at night so he doesn't chase the possums away.

376. If you get a lot of condensation inside your house, open windows for brief periods of time to allow dry air in and humid air to escape. Turn down the thermostat when you do this so that these brief exchanges of air won't use unnecessary energy. The latent heat in the structure will quickly compensate for the change, and then you can reset the thermostat in about 20 minutes.

377. If you are bothered by too much condensation on your windows, install storm windows or new double pane units.

378. If your bathroom gets really humid, it's better to open a window than run the fan for long period of time to get rid of condensation and humidity. In the winter you might just open the door, but in summer you don't want the humidity in the house, so open a window.

379. If you live in an area with hard water, mineral deposits can build up in the bottom of your water heater where the heat exchanger is, slowing it down and reducing efficiency. Open the faucet on the tank once a month and drain out one or two gallons of water to prevent mineral build up.

380. When you take a shower in winter, close the drain and let the water fill the tub. Drain the tub when the water has cooled, giving all of its warmth to your house. You will also benefit from a slight increase in humidity.

381. If you have Venetian blinds, adjust them in winter to face towards the sun. The sun will warm the blinds and the heat will be radiated into your home.

382. Another solution for too much in-house humidity is to install a "whole-house heat recovery system." This type of unit absorbs the heat from air being expelled and transfers that heat to dry incoming air. These units can also filter and purify the air at the same time.

383. Using the back of your hand to sense for cold air, go around your house and check all of the electrical, phone, and cable TV outlets. If you can feel cold air coming in, take the cover off and investigate for obvious gaps and holes you can block with sealer or caulk. Some hardware stores sell kits for this purpose. You may want to use foam insulation for bigger holes. Be careful never to touch live electrical wires.

384. The next time you have your furnace cleaned by professionals, ask them to check the delay settings on the temperature sensing switch. You may have heard the burner ignite and then the fan come on later. That's because the switch delays the fan until the burner is up to the specified temperatures. If it waits too long, that wastes energy.

385. Look under your kitchen and bathroom sinks, and behind your toilets to see where plumbing passes through walls. You will inevitably find some holes that are much bigger than the pipe that passes through them. Not only can insects get into your home this way, so will outside air, and that means wasted energy. Plug them up with caulking or sealer. Now you know why you always seem to have spiders in the bathroom and kitchen.

386. If you have automatic entry door closers, ensure that they close the door quickly after you are inside. If the door is held open for too long, too much outdoor air gets inside, making your HVAC work that much harder. These kinds of devices can change operation depending on temperatures, so check on them when it's really hot or cold.

387. To most efficiently water your garden and lawn on hot summer days, use a soaker hose. Too much water is lost to evaporation with a sprinkler system.

388. Many plants don't like for their leaves to get wet, roses especially. Water only the ground around the base of plants and keep the leaves dry. Better yet, use a drip system on a regulated timer.

389. You probably use surge protectors for your computer; if you don't, you are risking big repair bills or the loss of equipment. If you live in an area where lightning storms occur, you have to protect your computer, TV, stereo, in fact, all of your electronics. It may be cheaper to get a whole-house surge protector installed. Ask your hardware store or electrician for details.

390. Teflon pans are great for non-stick cooking, but they may be bad for your health, and they are an ongoing

and unnecessary expense when they need replacing. A seasoned cast iron pot or pan works almost as well as a non-stick, and cast iron is known for better "browning" of meats and foods like French toast. You can buy pre-seasoned cast iron pots and pans for a fraction of the price of Teflon coated ones, and you will never, ever have to replace them if they receive normal use and care.

391. If your toilet doesn't flush well, try putting white vinegar in the overflow tube in the tank. It will loosen hard water deposits on the flush jet and, hopefully, clear it. If that doesn't work, you will have to locate the flush jet inside the bowl and clean it out with a wire.

392. If a drain or toilet gets plugged, don't reach for the phone and call a plumber. Instead, get a plumber's friend (also known as a plunger). This handy device is available in most hardware and home improvement stores.

393. If a plunger can't unclog that sink or toilet, try using a garden hose to blast out the clog. Pack wet rags around the hose to build pressure and force the clog through.

394. Your toilets are often the biggest consumers of water in your home. Make sure they flush well. Installing a new water-efficient toilet to replace a troublesome older

model will make everyone happy and more than pay for itself in the long run.

If your sink drain plugs up, don't call a plumber. Buy a "plumber's friend" at the hardware store and try that first. If you are handy you could use a "snake." If you are careful, you can use a garden hose to "push" the drain clear. If you are plumbing capable, you can take apart the trap and clean it out. As a last resort remove the sink trap and clean it out. Don't forget a bucket to catch the sewage water that will leak out as soon as you loosen the fittings.

395. Most faucets are quickly repaired with a new washer that costs less than three dollars and you can easily do the job yourself. If you aren't sure how, ask the person at the hardware store for instructions or get a how-to book. It's not that difficult, requires only basic tools, and you will save hundreds of dollars in plumber bills. If you have to keep fixing a particular faucet with new washers, the seat is probably ruined and you should replace the seat or the whole faucet. Now that's a job for a plumber.

Save Money on Special Occasion Gifts and Other "Necessities"

396. Don't let your kids watch cartoons on Saturday mornings. They will hit you up for all the things they just saw on the commercials and you'll probably end up having to say "yes" to something you don't want to buy.

397. Spend less on your children's toys. So many toys are played with only briefly and then ignored or discarded. That's the truth of most children's toy boxes. Kids learn the wrong lesson about life when you buy them all this stuff that just sits around collecting dust. Kids are amazing; they will play with whatever they have at hand. You don't need to indulge them to have happy kids. It's more important to save for their future than it is to buy toys they will use once and forget about.

398. When buying gifts for children, less is often more. The things that delight children and keep their interest the longest are usually the "classics" like checkers, chess, baseball, football, dolls and tea sets. The latest "new" thing in toys is often the most expensive and will lose its luster quickly. Stick with lower priced classics.

399. Don't buy gifts for your kids that require consumables like batteries or cartridges. If you must buy battery

powered gifts, invest in a rechargeable battery system and make sure your kids use it. If you buy electronic games that require cartridges, look for ways to sell or exchange the ones in which they've lost interest. There are game stores that trade in such things, and you can also look for vendors at on-line sources and swap meets.

400. Even though your kids are begging "Santa" for the latest and greatest, don't buy the "hot" new electronic games when they are hot. Instead, look for used versions of the most popular games from months or years past. Just because Sony has a new PlayStation, or Microsoft has a new version of the X-box, doesn't mean the older versions aren't any fun. If your kids have never had a PlayStation or X-box, get them a used version of an older model and save tons of money. The cartridges are much cheaper too.

401. If you plan to have more than one child, buy unisex clothing of good quality so it will make a good "hand-me down" for the next one. Given good care, quality kids clothing, especially outerwear, can possibly survive through two or three kids.

402. Are you having a special occasion for your kids? Don't buy expensive "designer" clothes. Make them yourself,

or ask grandma or auntie to make them and they will be treasured well beyond childhood.

403. Does your employer recycle paper and cardboard? Ask if you can take discarded paper and cardboard for your kids to use for drawing, crafts and fun stuff.

404. Give gifts that you know the recipient would buy for themselves. If your spouse has a yearning to buy something, and you know that eventually they will go ahead and get it anyway even though it's not in the family budget, surprise them and buy it for them on their birthday or as a holiday gift.

405. If you are hosting a holiday dinner, cook it yourself, and ask your relatives to bring what they can to help out. Going out to a restaurant for meals or hiring a catering service is the most expensive option around the holidays or any other day. And if you are the host, it will save you the expense of driving to someone else's place during the holidays and you get to keep all the leftovers!

406. If you do have to drive to visit relatives during the holiday season, carpool with other relatives who live near you if you have to travel a long distance. The kids will have a great time and you'll save on gas.

407. Wherever there are groups of people who exchange gifts during the holidays, for example, the office, school or clubs, gift giving can get out of hand and cost you a bundle. Instead, initiate a "Secret Santa" where everyone draws a name out of a hat and gives that person a gift anonymously. Everyone receives a gift. No one has to buy a gift for everyone.

408. You can also start a "not-so-secret-Santa" for your relatives. Think of the money you would save if you only had to buy just one of your relatives a gift. Get them all together and agree on a spending limit, then draw names out of a hat to see who is giving a gift to whom. Make a list of the things you would want that fit the budget, and send it to your not-so-secret Santa. You might as well be practical while you are at it and ask for something you would have bought yourself anyway. Need a new drill or flower vase? Now's your chance.

409. Bottom line for gift giving: you must have a budget and you and your spouse must both stick to it. Sometimes the best surprise is no surprises. Amaze your spouse with a savings bond or a big deposit to your financial security plan. Wrap it up and give it as a gift. They will love you for it, especially if you are the "spender" in the family.

410. Never buy holiday decorations - make them yourself! Wreaths, center pieces, ornaments and garlands can all be creatively made at home rather than purchased at a store. It will give your home a special look that is all your own and will delight those who visit. For example, a little tin foil, some popcorn, some string and a little food coloring can make a fancy garland. A candle, some branches, a few pine cones, and a few fall-colored leaves and berries can make a centerpiece. Use your imagination or look through some holiday issues of home and crafts magazines at the library for ideas.

411. If you work in a store and can get extra hours at holiday pay, go for it. You and your family can celebrate the day before or the day after the "actual" day. It's all made up anyway. The biggest challenge is letting go of old traditions and starting new ones. Do something special with half the extra money and save the rest.

412. Outdoor lighting is festive and makes your house glow for the holidays. It's also expensive to light up all those bulbs. Use smaller wattage bulbs wherever you can, and keep the number of lights to a minimum. Put them on a timer so you don't leave them on all night. You don't need to be the best decorated house in the neighborhood for Santa to find you. Just a small or modest display will

keep the holiday spirit going; it doesn't take much. Keep it simple and save your money for all those holiday bills you will get in January.

413. A living Christmas tree that can be used for several years may be cheaper than a cut tree that hits the trash bin on New Year's Day. An artificial tree may last many years, but they can be expensive initially and go out of style or deteriorate with age. Look for the best compromise that costs you the least amount of money. If you do buy a cut tree, get it from a local service organization and write it off as a holiday donation.

414. Put your holiday decorations away carefully. For many of us, when the holidays are over we just want to get "all this stuff" out of sight as quickly as possible. A little bit of care packing it away for next year can save you money you will inevitably have to spend replacing broken lights, ornaments and decorations.

415. Do your holiday shopping early during the year when there are sales. Prices get higher as the holidays grow closer. Next year, start a budget in January for holiday gifts you will buy in August, September, October, and November. A little planning can save you a ton of money, and not only that, you will have a lot less stress around the holidays!

416. Do your gift shopping in the months before the holidays when things really do go on sale. Sales during the holidays are often loss-leaders to get you into the stores to buy.

417. Never go for the latest "breakthrough" products that are always sold at a premium, no matter how badly you want them. Last year's electronics, cameras, computers, TV's and video gear are often nearly as good, sometimes better, than this year's models and sell at a fraction of the cost.

418. Ni-cad rechargeable batteries like those in cordless phones, small appliances and tools, have a "memory" and that means they tend to run down quicker the more you use them. To "erase" their memory, let them run completely down every month or two. They will last longer, too.

419. Most of these devices have a black transformer or similar device that plugs into the wall a/c outlet to charge them. Unplug these transformers when you aren't charging the batteries; they use current even when they aren't charging batteries.

420. Every month let rechargeable batteries totally run down before recharging them. This way they will not develop

the memory of the slightly-discharged state and you will be able to get the full charge of electricity out of them when you need it. This can also significantly increase the battery life.

Save Money with Babies, Toddlers, and Young Children

421. Make your own baby food. Bottled, processed baby food is a waste of money. Making your own is easy to do, and it's better for baby too. A food processor and a strainer are all you need to make healthful, nutritious food for your baby that is far superior nutritionally to anything that comes in a jar.

422. Make your own kids' toys. There are hundreds of fun things you can make practically for free right at home that will entertain your kids for hours and hours. Check out the hundreds of ideas at http://www.allthingsfrugal. com/kids.htm.

423. First-time parents tend to over-react and over-indulge their first born. If you or someone you know are about to become first-time parents, get some advice from an "experienced" parent with two or more kids, but it needs to be someone whose judgment you trust. Ask them for coaching and advice in exchange for something of

value you could offer in return. 24/7 phone support would be good to ask for…just kidding! Remember your goal is to save money. This idea alone could save you thousands, not to mention giving you a big dose of peace-of-mind.

424. Hand-me-down clothes seem like such an obvious way to save money, but the truth is kids' clothes get pretty beat up and only the best survive. That means you want to look in places where only the best would do--a garage sale in a trendy area like Palm Beach or Beverly Hills, for example. Or, if you have wealthy relatives or friends, ask them to share the wealth before they send those unwanted baby items to the trash or to charity.

425. Disposable diapers are great because they are so convenient, but "reusable" diapers are the way to go when you are in a money saving mindset. What could you do with around $1,000 savings per child? That's the bottom-line cost difference between disposable and reusable "nappies." Yes, you do get used to it!

426. Babies outgrow their clothes, and they also outgrow their cribs just as quickly. Why not start with something they can grow into? A child size bed will work just as well as a crib if you plan it out from the beginning, and

you won't have wasted money for a crib. Be creative! Be frugal!

427. Shoes-- we don't need no stinking shoes! Babies hate 'em, parents for some reason think they need them, especially first-time parents. Ask your "baby coach," but we'd bet socks and covers will do just fine in those first months. It's shocking to think some "designer" baby shoes cost nearly $100! Wow! But, hey, they look great in bronze!

428. Baby shampoo, cotton wipes, bath soap and all that special stuff "just for baby" is cheaper in its generic form. Much cheaper. You really pay through the nose for those brand label baby toiletries, and it can add up fast. Generic's the name of the game.

429. Don't pay a fortune for a couple years' supply of "wipes" when a washcloth will do. No one likes to do a lot of laundry, but when you have a baby you just get used to it. You will save money, lots of money, by using old fashioned cotton washcloths and hand towels instead of disposable wipes. What did people do before they invented these things anyway? You'll survive!

Even More Ways to Save Money:

430. A bargain is a bargain only if you can use it.

431. Keep a record of what you spend and compare month to month. This will help you track your spending habits so you can make changes where necessary.

432. Always be savings conscious. For instance, even though you may not need gasoline at the moment, keep an eye open for where the best prices are as you drive around.

433. Remember: small savings on small items add up over time.

434. Take advantage of government services… after all you pay for them! Let the library be your bookstore… you'll never pay for a book again. Many have books on tape, books on CD, and some even loan DVD's.

435. If you freeze candles before lighting them, they will burn much longer.

436. Don't answer your phone around dinner time because it almost always is a salesperson trying to sell you something you don't need.

437. Never pay retail. Only buy discretionary items when they are on sale. Clothes, shoes, appliances, TV's, computers, cameras, cars, trucks… all of these kinds of consumer goods frequently go on sale. You should never pay retail

price for any of these kinds of items. Every time you do, you miss an opportunity to save and build wealth.

438. Internet resources such as eBay are wonderful channels for getting bargains on items that you would otherwise have to pay retail. "Warehouse" volume discounters like Price Club, Best Buy or Costco offer everyday goods at great prices when you buy larger quantities. Just don't get carried away and buy more than you need or can use.

439. A low-mileage used car or truck that is two or three years old is always a far greater value than a new one. Do your research. Buy for good resale value, economy, reliability and low maintenance, not for dazzle and style. New cars lose up to 10% of their value the moment they're driven off the lot by the new owner. The most expensive makes and models can lose up to 25% of their value in just a few months of ownership.

440. Consistently shop around for the best prices for gasoline, food and household needs, and you can add hundreds--if not thousands--of dollars a year to your savings that will compound into even greater wealth in the future.

441. When you get your hair cut, have it cut shorter and let it grow out longer. You can cut in half what you pay

for haircuts each year using this strategy. Better yet, ask your spouse, friend, or a relative to cut your hair. Be sure to return the favor.

442. When you travel with kids, always look out for signs that say "kids stay free" or "kids' meals are free."

443. When you need new furniture, it's always cheaper if you buy it used from a private party. Since it is expensive to ship furniture, look for used furniture in local classified ads and at garage sales or swap meets in or near higher income neighborhoods.

444. If you can't find what you want through the classifieds or garage sales, buy furniture directly from the manufacturer and transport it yourself, or better yet, buy unfinished furniture and finish it yourself.

445. Always protect your upholstered furniture with a spray-on fabric protector. You will need to renew the process about once a year.

446. If the fabric on your couch wears out, fades or goes out of style, but the rest of the couch is in good condition, consider recovering with new fabric, or buy a form fitted cover in a material that suits you better.

447. Get into the habit of returning things. That means you have to keep careful track of your receipts. If you buy something and end up not using it, rather than let it sit on the shelf forever, take it back for a refund.

448. Shop for electronics or similar high-tech items at membership warehouse stores with liberal refund policies. You could, for example, buy an electronic device that goes bad months after the warranty has expired, and still be able to return it for a full refund… but only if you've kept the original boxes and the receipt.

449. If you like to send cards for almost every occasion, buy assorted cards in bulk at a discount store, planning ahead for the year. Not only will you save money on the cards, you won't have to make so many trips to the card shop. Don't buy more than you need--that's just wasting money.

450. To save money on cards altogether, make your own cards using an inkjet printer and one of the many "free" sites on the internet, like www.hallmark.com.

451. Besides saving your loose change in a jar, try saving all your $1 and $5 bills as well. Once you get in the habit, you won't miss them, and seeing bills and coins pile up in a jar is very inspiring.

452. When you want to make a major purchase (anything over $50) save up enough money to buy it at full retail price. When you actually go to buy it, look for the best price you can get. After you get it as a "bargain," put the difference into your savings jar and pat yourself on the back. Let's say you want a new lamp and it costs $150. You save up the full $150 and then find that if you just wait two weeks, the lamp will go on sale for half price. You'd pay $75 for the lamp, and put the other $75 into your savings.

453. When you find a "big ticket" item that you really need, always ask when it will go on sale. Most sales people know this information, and they will tell you if you ask. You might have to wait a week or a month, but you will save $$$s by waiting for a sale.

454. When you buy electronics or anything that comes in a box with a manual, be sure to save not only your receipt, but the box and the manual. When you don't need it anymore and you want to sell it on eBay or at a garage sale, you will get a much higher price if you have the original box, manual, and receipt. This will also make it much easier to return something for repair, especially if it's still under the warranty, so it's a good habit to get into.

455. Turn clothes inside out when washing and drying. This will help keep the color fast and won't wear out the "beauty" side of your garments.

456. Whenever you buy clothes, take the time to inspect each garment and check for imperfections. A sweater with a "pull" in the fabric, a shirt that doesn't fit quite right, a dress with a missing button, a suit with misaligned seams...these are not "bargains." Defects are to be expected, if not tolerated as the norm, at outlet stores, so you need to be especially careful there.

457. Find a good dry cleaner that won't wreck your clothes. Nothing will ruin a good suit faster than a cheap dry cleaner. Develop a relationship with your dry cleaner so that they know you by name. Thank them for their high quality work and let them know how much you appreciate that they take good care of your clothes. That way when something happens to your clothes, you can get a good response from them concerning repair or replacement.

458. Start a car pool where you drive other people to work and charge them for the ride. When you take your kids to school, charge other parents to take theirs, too. On weekends, offer rides for friends and neighbors to and from the mall. You may have to get a limousine permit

if business gets too good. Be sure your auto insurance covers the passengers in your vehicle.

459. If you have cats and dogs, you'll need flea and tick medicine. If you get them through the vet, they are very expensive. Look for sources on-line or through mail-order.

460. Check with your local pet shops for low-cost "clinics." Many stores will hold clinics over the weekend and you can get vet attention for your pet at greatly reduced prices.

461. If you have an "emergency" with your pet, in many areas you can take them to the local SPCA and get emergency help for free or at very low cost. Check with your local SPCA ahead of time so you know what their policies are and any emergency number you might want to keep on hand.

462. Keeping older animals alive well past their natural lifespan can be very expensive, and in some cases borders on cruelty. You want to carefully weigh your emotional attachment with your pet's needs. Talk to your vet about when it's time to let them go. Get clear financial assessments regarding your pet's health and

what it will really take over the long run to keep them healthy.

463. Boarding your pet is too expensive, and it is likely that they will be stressed and exposed to any number of diseases. Instead, hire a friend or neighbor to look after your pet in their familiar home setting. You'll save money and your pet will be healthier and happier.

464. Bathe and groom your pet yourself. Pet grooming services are expensive, and a waste of money for something you can easily do yourself.

465. Like most Americans, many pets are overweight. Overweight pets lose their health quickly. Not only does all that extra food cost more, when your pet gets sick, treatment can be a heavy expense. Many veterinarians believe that pets get all the nutrients they need from dry pet food, and it's often less expensive than moist varieties. You don't need to buy moist food for cats or dogs. Realize that it's harder to discipline yourself than it is to get your pet to eat dry food. When they get hungry enough, they'll eat.

466. Keep the ashtray in your car completely full of quarters. Consider it your little stash of "abundance." The next time you need money for the parking meter, you'll have

a good supply of quarters on hand. You should never get a parking ticket again.

467. Many people put bottles and cans with a redemption value in the recycle bin, or worse yet, the trash. Turn them in for cash and put the money in your savings jar.

468. You get the most toothpaste for your money in an old fashioned roll up tube. If you are roll it up carefully as you use it, you can get almost all the toothpaste out. Be sure to always put the lid on so you don't waste it.

469. Never put more toothpaste on the brush than you need. Toothpaste isn't good for kids to ingest, so teach them to use only a small amount. This not only saves on money for toothpaste, but more importantly it is better for your child's health. Many people are surprised there is a health warning on a box of toothpaste. Make sure they don't swallow it if at all possible – and get in the habit of only using a small amount.

470. Always use rechargeable batteries whenever possible. They are much cheaper to use even than alkaline batteries because they are reusable many times over.

471. Sell anything you've had in storage for more than a year and never even looked at. If you haven't needed it in a

year's time, you don't need it at all. Sell those items and turn them into savings. Exceptions: family heirlooms, photos, and memories, but let's face it, even those don't usually take up enough room to justify a storage unit. The bottom line is you should never need a storage unit for more than a year.

472. You can use "gray water" from your laundry, shower, tub, or bathroom sink to wash your car or truck. To do this you will need to install a diverter and a container to catch the gray water for later use.

473. Use a "push" mower to cut your lawn instead of a gas or electric powered unit. Not only will you save on expense for fuel or electricity, you'll get some good exercise.

474. If you have to have a power mower or riding mower, see if you can share the cost of one with your neighbors.

475. Grow fruit trees to enhance the value of your property and save on grocery bills. If you sell the excess at a roadside stand, put the proceeds in your savings jar.

476. Plant a "victory garden" just like many did during WWII and save on vegetables and produce. It worked then, and it still works today to save you $$$s.

477. How many pairs of reading glasses do you own? You only need one good pair, but you have to take very good care of them. Having several pairs of glasses because you frequently lose them, sit on them, or otherwise render them useless is a waste of money. Get a good pair of glasses, keep them in a hard case when you don't need them, and they will last for years. You will save money, perhaps hundreds of dollars.

478. When you buy a suit, get two pairs of pants to go with the coat. The coat will most likely outlast both of them and you'll get more service from the coat that way.

479. Don't leave mail in your mailbox for the letter carrier to pick up if there are checks, money, or confidential information in your letters. Thieves drive around ahead of the letter carriers looking for the raised red flags, and steal outgoing mail. They then take your checks and put their name as payee. Worse, if they get enough information, they can steal your identity!

480. When you drop letters into a letter box, always open the lid to make sure the letters dropped. You may think this silly or even paranoid, but actually it is quite common for mail thieves to put globs of sticky glue on the inside of the letter box lid. They may come back as innocent looking people simply mailing a letter, but they're really

looking for "stuck" letters to steal. The safest method is to take your "secure" mail directly to the post office.

481. Instead of taking a taxi to the airport on your next trip, ask a friend or neighbor to take you. Return the favor or pay it forward.

482. If you do drive yourself to the airport, how do you know you've found the cheapest parking? Obviously, it takes some research and planning, so you can't do it when you are late for your flight. Next time you are driving near your airport, take a little time to drive around and find the cheapest long term parking.

483. While you are there, find out how much short term parking costs compared to the lowest long term price. The next time you drop off a family member, you might want to park in the long term lot even though you are just seeing them off.

484. Plan your travel dates well in advance and buy your tickets early. Ticket prices climb exponentially as lead time grows short to buy your ticket.

485. The same is true for hotels. Book your rental car early as well, just in case there is a convention in town and all the cars are taken.

486. If you know you are traveling to a destination city on a certain date, go on-line and see if there are any conventions or big events happening at the same time you will be there. You might want to change your date as rates are much higher when the demand rises during a convention or big sporting event

487. If you have a real family emergency, you can get most airlines to give you discount prices on last minute tickets.

488. Buy used books. Even the hottest best sellers show up in used book stores at half price very quickly. When you buy used books you save money, but you should also take good care of the books you own so you can sell them back for the highest price possible – that means no torn covers, no dog-earring of pages, no food or water stains.

489. Do you like to "burn" CD's and DVD's in your computer? If you do, then you have undoubtedly made a bunch of "coasters" discs that didn't burn correctly and are unusable. Don't throw them away--use them for decorations, hang them in fruit trees to frighten the birds, use them as coasters for the table, or turn them into artwork. There are literally thousands of uses for CD and DVD "coasters."

490. You may like to print photos with your computer and a photo printer, but it's costing you five to ten times more than using a professional service to do it. If you have a digital camera, mark only the frames you want developed into prints as you preview them on your computer's screen. There are many internet services available, or you can burn a CD and take it to a developer. You might have to wait an hour or a day, but you will save lots of money.

491. Make your own greeting cards, birthday cards, anniversary cards, etc. You will save money, and people appreciate hand-made items more.

492. Buy your clothes at vintage shops, charity shops, and other second-hand shops. Also check out websites like eBay for second-hand clothing.

493. Need an expensive clothing item? Check eBay for the same item — even if you don't buy there, you'll know what the best price is, and you will have target for how much you should spend.

494. Can't wait until that new best selling book is available at the library? Purchase it for half price by sharing the cost — and the book — with a friend.

495. Check with the web sites of the manufacturers of your favorite shampoo, cereal or other products to see if you can download a cents-off coupon.

496. If you call a consumer products company's customer service line to ask a question, they will sometimes send you a free sample of their product.

497. Rebates aren't always publicized. Check the web sites of the retailer and the manufacturer of products you want to purchase to see if a rebate is offered.

498. When you apply for a rebate, keep track of them and make sure they actually come back to you. Many times you have to "tickle" the company to get your money. Write letters, get on the phone, and make them send you your money!

499. If you want to celebrate a special occasion or function by taking people out to eat, go to lunch instead of dinner. Restaurants charge much less for lunch than when the same entrée is offered at dinner time.

500. Don't order dessert or coffee at the end of a restaurant meal. Instead, wait until you get home to have a slice of pie and avoid the high mark-up restaurants charge on these extras.

501. Be careful not to let your parking meter run out of time. Municipalities that need cash charge exorbitant fines. Tie a string around your finger, put a note in your wallet, or set the alarm on your cell phone to remind you when you need to put more money in the meter.

502. Replace the filters on your car's engine regularly, and be sure to keep it tuned. A new oxygen sensor alone can improve gas mileage by as much as 15 percent.

503. Keep your tires properly inflated. Under-inflated tires can result in loss in gas mileage as high as 5 percent.

504. Can't give up bottled water? Consider getting a home cooler. The initial payout is steep (as much as $150 to $200) but a 5-gallon jug costs around $5, compared with $1 per pint for individual bottles from the local grocery.

505. Have a yard sale. You get rid of things you don't need, and can add the money to your stash of loose change and $1 and $5 bills.

506. Keep your dollars in your pocket for ten days before you spend them. You will receive a new understanding of the value of your money. It will become a part of you and you will feel uncomfortable when it is not there.

507. Study the money course found on www.NADFA.com.

508. Act on just one idea that you found in this book! One great idea can change your future and make retirement prosperous.

509. Act on two ideas that you found in this book! Two ideas used together will magnify the result exponentially.

510. Act on three ideas that you found in this book! Three ideas combined with action will have your friends and neighbors clamoring to do what you are doing.

511. Act on four or five ideas that you found in this book! Your friends will think you are a genius.

512. Order the book *Debt Hurts* from www.AuthorHouse. com.

513. Visit www.PowerProgram.com.

Printed in the United States
73555LV00002B/421-486